glimpses

for those who do not believe
for those who need their belief encouraged

S T E P H E N   G I O R D A N O

ISBN 978-1-68517-830-7 (paperback)
ISBN 978-1-68517-831-4 (digital)

Christian Faith Publishing
832 Park Avenue
Meadville, PA 16335
www.christianfaithpublishing.com

Printed in the United States of America

To
GOD THE FATHER
GOD THE SON
GOD THE HOLY SPIRIT

Special love and prayerful thanks to
Donna, my wife,
for her constant praying for me, her boundless love, and her great faith
and unending support—truly a blessing from GOD in my life.
The late Senior Pastor Richard Bruschi,
founder of Freedom Road Bible Church.
Pastor Richard Bruschi II.
Pastor William Gillispie.

May these writings prayerfully become a legacy to my grandchildren—
that they may all come to know CHRIST in their lives.

To be a blessing in the life of another is the greatest thing that one can be.

Steve

You, the reader, will find that there are many words throughout this work that are in capitals, when they are used to refer to the DIVINE. This is done out of respect and reverence for GOD the FATHER, GOD the SON, our LORD and SAVIOR JESUS CHRIST, and GOD the HOLY SPIRIT.

At the heart of this endeavor has always been my belief that these entries are from THEM in order to reach out to you.

Contained within these pages are many years of starts and stops along the path of faith, with success and failures, reflections, and journeys of the SPIRIT.

I believe that HIS purpose in this manuscript is so that HIS heart can reach out to others who find themselves lost to belief, new to belief, growing in belief, or have come to a crossroad or a standstill in their belief.

Although this is not a daily devotional in that there are not three hundred sixty-five readings, it is suggested that you, the reader, take time to journey through slowly, to pause and reflect and think. What the BIBLE refers to as *SELAH*, "*to pause and think on these things.*"

Take the time to internalize and make these words yours and their meanings yours. May the writings herein speak to you as messages to you from HIM.

Contents

An Introduction

May I introduce you to someone?
Someone beyond great,
For HE is greatness.
Someone beyond any love,
For HE is love itself.
Someone greater than your world,
For HE created it.
Someone awe-inspiring, majestic.
Someone who has the desire
To free you
From all bondage.
To heal you
Physically, mentally, emotionally.
To sustain you
Body, mind, spirit.
To save you
From all sin,
Past, present, future.

Would you like to meet HIM?
HE is waiting for you
To come to HIM.

What do I have to do?
Nothing, HE wants to meet you
Just as you are.

Where do I have to go?
Nowhere, HE is right here
With you right now.

What words do I use?
No words, HE already knows
Everything about you.

Just tell HIM, ***"Here I am"***
HE will take it from there.

God's Love—a Glimpse

God's love is diverse, as awesome, as powerful, as HE is HIMSELF.
God has love for us, gives love to us, is love to us.

God's love goes beyond human love.
God's love can look upon us with sorrow and pity,
Resigned to do what HE must do in our lives.
God's love can look upon us with joy and exaltation,
With pride when we manifest HIS great love.

How does God look at me, I wonder?
HE sees me as I am and loves me.
HE sees me as HE wants me to be and loves me.
HE sees the good and bad sides of me and loves me.
HE loves the me that I sometimes do not.

HE loves those that we do not.
HE loves those that the world does not.
HE loves those the world says are unlovable.
HE loves the lost, the forgotten, the hurting.
HE loves directly and loves through others.

Oh! That we could manifest God's love to all.
HE wants us to give our love
And after we have given it all
HE will give us HIS love to give.

For that is what HE did.
HE gave HIS love
Then HE gave his love
Lastly, HE gave HIS love.
For you see,
God's love, even a glimpse, is endless.

God's Kind of Love

There is a kind of love
That only GOD can know,
That only HE can have.

A love that always loves
No matter what
No matter where
No matter how
No matter why.

Love based on nothing
Except that HE loves you.

No matter what you are
No matter where you are
No matter who you are
No matter what you have done
No matter why you did it.

GOD loves you because
You are and HE IS.

GOD loves with love
That is different from ours.
No agenda and nothing in return.

Even if you don't love HIM back
This changes nothing.
GOD still loves you
With a kind of love
That only HE can know,
That only HE can have.

But, loving HIM back couldn't hurt!

A Thought of You

If a thought will make YOU real to me
Then I will think of YOU always.
If a song could release YOUR love
Then I would sing unceasingly.
If a picture is worth a thousand words
Then I will paint a picture of YOU with my heart.
For then a thousand words of YOU
Would dwell in my heart always.

A picture, the words, a song, the thoughts
Held in my heart
Would not fade with age.
But become a brighter picture,
Truer words,
A sweeter song,
Stronger thoughts.

Oh, that these would fill the rooms of my life
Hang in my heart
Give rest to my mind
Surround my soul.

May these thoughts of YOU
Words of YOUR love
Songs of YOUR salvation
Pictures of YOUR presence
Be eternal and live on past my life.

May others by THY will
Think of YOU
Sing of YOU
Paint their own picture of YOU
To fill their hearts
With YOU.

For You

I created you out of nothing
So I could give you everything.

From the dust of the earth
To the eternity of heaven.

From feeding thousands physically
To feeding countless millions spiritually.

To feeding you;
Yes, you individually.

Feeding your higher needs,
The needs of your spirit.

You can be truly filled
In so many ways, so many levels.

You can be truly filled,
But only by ME.

For MY *filling is true filling.*
It takes you from being poor in SPIRIT.
To being rich in MY *presence.*
For you

Give Me

Consider MY *love*
MY *love removes sorrow.*

Consider ME
Your LORD.

Give ME *the chance*
To come to you.

Give ME *the chance*
To show you MY *love.*

Give ME *the chance*
To draw you close to ME.

As you come to ME
Turn your face toward mine.

Give ME *the ability to see your face,*
Please do not turn your back on ME!

If you are lost
I will find you.

To find you
I must see your face.

Your back I do not recognize.
Look to ME.
Give ME *the chance.*

Give Me 2

Give ME *your ears that you may hear*
The sounds that I hear.
The sounds of MY *creation*
The praises it sings.

Give ME *your eyes that you may see*
The way I see.
The sights of MY *creation*
Show MY *presence.*

Give ME *your voice*
That I may speak through you.
To bring you dose to ME
That you may speak to others.

Give ME *your hands*
That I may do mighty works,
MY *way in* MY *time*
At MY *discretion.*

Give ME *your legs*
That I may send you to your knees.
From your knees you arise,
Go out, into the world.

Give ME *your Soul, your Spirit,*
They are mine anyway.
For they came from ME,
Are part of ME.

Now I can bless them
And give them to you again.
Pure, whole, restored.
Just give ME *the chance.*

Grace

Almighty GOD took HIMSELF from eternity
Compressed HIMSELF into a span of time
Into the nature of a servant.
Grace.

So that HE could teach, heal, reveal
HIS grace we could see, hear, feel.
Directly, personally, intimately.
Grace.

After all this, HE gave HIMSELF
The final sacrifice.
Grace.

Love and grace not just shown
But given.
So we could understand, possess.
Grace.

Teach Me

LORD, teach me to love
The way YOU love.
Built on nothing
But love itself.
Love for love's sake only.

Teach me to forgive,
The way YOU forgive.
Forgiveness without counting wrongs.
The forgiveness of forgetting.
Knowing transgressions no longer matter.

Teach me to show mercy and grace,
The way YOU show.
For YOU more than show,
YOU give these to me,
YOU place them upon me as a garment.

Teach me to praise YOU.
Teach me to worship YOU.
That this small act
Is pleasing to YOU.
For no reason other than that alone.

Teach me how to bless YOU, LORD.
That I may show a meager appreciation
For all the blessings
Seen and unseen,
YOU have given me.

His Will

His will for you is vast.
Impossible to comprehend.
Able to affect and move
The entire universe.
Your life; each life,
For you.

His will encompasses
All time, all space.
All days, each moment.
All events, all circumstances.
All thoughts, all actions.
Past, present, future.

His will weaves
The seen and unseen.
From a drop of rain
To the spin of a star.
The quietest prayer
May alter creation.

Such is HIS way
For you
His will.

Obedience

Obedience
Is not a bad word.
CHRIST was obedient to the FATHER.

Obedience
Of which we may be reluctant at first,
Grows into real faith.

Obedience
May take you from the rough path
To the smooth one.

Obedience
Can take paths of tears,
Removes your fears.

Obedience
Finds you lost
And takes you home.

Obedience
Brings you through
Trial, sadness, burdens.

Obedience
Is the quiet voice.
HIS guidance, HIS Word, HIS SPIRIT.

Obedience
Docile yet strong.
Submissive yet overpowering.

Obedience
Is HIS rod and HIS staff.
They comfort you.

No, obedience is not a bad word.

One Moment in Time

The most powerful event in all history!
One moment of victorious time.
Touched each and every person
Past, present, future.
You are changed by this one moment in time
Regardless if you believe or not.

CHRIST arose from death to life.
A difficult concept to grasp.
To those of faith, it is not a concept
But truth based on belief.
An actual event proven by the SPIRIT.

CHRIST took all sin
To the grave with HIM.
Left them buried and forgotten.
Returned victorious and free.

If CHRIST is not risen
In that one moment in time
Then GOD is dead is the result.

If CHRIST is not risen
We are forever lost,
Condemned and bound.
HIS purpose in coming forth from the FATHER
Was all in vain.

If this were to be true
Then the entire Word of GOD is a lie.
Preachers, teachers, believers living that lie.
Therefore, our faith is false and worthless.

To believe in the resurrection,
Forgiveness from sin,
Life eternal,
To become real and true for you,
All it takes is one moment in time.

The only difference is that
This time,
It is your time.

He Stands

The Lord stands just outside your door,
Awaiting your invitation
To enter your life.

Will you invite him in?
Humbly bow down?
Obeying his lordship,
His life in you.

Or will he enter unannounced?
As an unwanted judge
With his righteous conviction.

Do you hear him?
There, just outside your door?
Listen, obey, open, and live.

Or refuse to hear,
Refuse to obey,
Lock the door.

If so, you have lost a chance!
Grace ignored,
Mercy slipped by.

You pronounce your own doom!
Do not throw away your chance.
Open your door.

He awaits your obedience
Just outside your door
With another chance.

If you open the door to your heart
You will find that there—
Waiting, he stands!

Time

Before time began,
Now in time's midst;
After time ends,
I AM!

Before time began
Has no meaning to you.
After time ends
Has no meaning for you.

Here in time's midst
Is where you are
And where you are,
I AM!

Yes, I AM with you
In your mountaintop times.
Yes, I AM with you
In your dry, desert times.

Seasons of time pass:
Years, months, weeks; days, hours.
They come to and go away.
All to bring you to ME.

You are in time, I AM not.
But time is here, time is now
To make you Mine.

Time passes only forward.
Take this time here and now
Before your time ends
To come to ME.

Time is
And time is not.
At both ends of time,
I AM!

Two Trees

At the first tree
Sin begins.
At the second tree
Sin ends.

At the first tree
Man falls.
At the second tree
Man arises.

The living tree
brought death.
The dead tree
Brings life.

To take of the first tree
We die.
To take of the second tree
We live.

Because of the first tree
When we are born
We are destined to die.

Because of the second tree
When we die
We are destined to live.

The first tree
Took us out of paradise.
The second tree
Takes us into paradise.

The first tree
Brings life to an end.
The second tree
Brings eternal life.

Two Caves

In one cave, heaven came to man,
In the other cave, man returned to heaven.

One cave beheld a HIM wrapped in cloths,
The other cave held HIM wrapped in cloths of the grave.

From each cave came life, grace, and hope.
Both caves hold the promise for a future.

Enter in, take hold of what both caves have for you.
Both caves offer you the promise of MESSIAH!

Out of one cave came the gospel and healing,
Out of the other came redemption and salvation.

Both caves are to be a part of your life.
You must go from knowing one cave to enter the other.

Do not just walk past but enter and explore the two caves,
See what each holds for you.
For in between these two caves
Lies the span of your life.

Both caves have a wonderful life to offer you.
One cave holds the secret to life here and now,
The other holds the secret to life after and forever.

Discover the one cave that starts your new life here.
To find the other cave that starts your new life there.
Two caves.

Two Gates, Two Paths

Matthew 7:13–14

For Pastor Rick, who shows us the gates and where the paths may lead us

Two gates, two paths.
Wide gate, wide path.
Narrow gate, narrow path.

The easy one is the wide path,
The hard one is the narrow path.
One gate opens to the world,
The other gate opens to the realm of SPIRIT.

They lead not to the same destination.
One leads to the world's desires,
One leads to the desires of SPIRIT.
Your life cannot walk two paths.

The wide path has more gates along the way.
Gates both wide and narrow.
For as you walk along, choices call out.
You can always change the path you're on.

Likewise, the narrow path has more wide gates.
These are the wide-open gates of temptation,
Trying to pull you off the narrow path.

Walk the narrow path with faith.
See the wide gates get few and far between
They disappear completely.

Now you are only on the narrow path.
The wide path is for everyone,
The narrow path is now for you.

The narrow gate opens only by acceptance,
It is the gate behind HIS cross.
The wide gate, nothing blocks,
It stands open, easy to enter in.

Choose a gate, choose a path.
CHRIST gives you that freedom.
The gate you enter, the path you walk,
Is up to you.

Or

Mark 5:27–29, 34

Do you want to watch JESUS walk past,
If only to touch the hem of HIS garment as HE passes?
Or
Would you rather come boldly
And be open, come, seek, ask

To simply receive one blessing
And go on with your life?
Or
To come forward
Show your faith, your trust.

To go from the outer things of GOD,
Which is HIS hem to you
Or
To enter the inner things of GOD,
Which becomes HIM touching you.

You in HIM starts your journey of faith,
To go forward in life, in peace.
And
HIM in you requires HIS supremacy.
HIM healing you now and forever.

There is a world of difference between the two,
An eternal world.

Prayer Is Taking the Time

A benefit of prayer is not always in the asking,
Not even in the receiving,
But the act itself.
This is prayer.

Taking the time
To sit, kneel, stand, or recline.
Taking time to simply be.
Taking time for communion.
Communion not of action or word.

Just to be.
Willing to receive nothing,
As well as give nothing.
Just to be at rest
From oneself and the world.

With soul set free,
Your spirit and HIS
Neither saying anything
Just being together
In the quiet.

It is possible
To be with GOD
To listen without hearing
To speak without words.
Lifting your heart.

Take the time
To lighten your mind,
To rest in HIS love.
This too is prayer,
Taking the time.

Did They See?

Did they see, o LORD, did they know
The things HE would do, the things HE would show?
Did she see, o LORD, did Mary see
Her infant SON would die for me?
This little babe upon her breast
Would die for my eternal rest.
The wise men, o LORD, did they see
Whom they beheld is the KING of GLORY?
Did they see, know, or even wonder
This little child created the dawn and the thunder?
Did he see, o LORD, did Joseph know
As he watched his small boy grow,
Trained HIM in the carpenter there
Did he see, LORD, have HIS cross to bear?
As HE grew, o LORD and played with HIS friends
Did they see HIS love would never end?
Did they see HIS child's arms open wide
As a man to accept the cross as HE died?
As a man, o LORD, with HIS disciples around
Didn't they see the dead arise from the ground?
Did they see, o LORD, or even care
That one day JESUS would no longer be there?
Did they see, o LORD, or even know
That He was showing them the way to go?
At the tomb, o LORD, did they understand
This is the beginning and not the end?
What of YOUR church, o LORD, help us to see
YOUR perfect will, love, and unity.
Unbelievers, o LORD, what do they see?
Man not GOD, flesh with no DIVINITY,
A curious fellow who lived and died
Who has nothing to do with who I am inside.
The future, o LORD, what do you see,
A world that is lost or on bended knee?
What of my family, o LORD, me and friends?
Well, we know, we'll see YOU when worldly sight ends.
For I know YOU are true, as is YOUR Word
And I praise the gospel, which thank GOD I've heard.
And the rest, o LORD, what will they see,
What will they learn, what will they say
On the day YOU return?
Do they see, o LORD, do they see what I see,
All the wonderous things you have done for me,
O LORD, do they see?

Joseph of Arimathea

Mark 15:43 and John 19:38

He asked for the body of Jesus.
He didn't ponder or suggest,
He came forward and asked.

Something inside him changed,
He took that step—from secret believer
To openly ask for Christ.

The death of Christ at the cross
Changed everything for him.
So he asked for Christ.

The cross caused him to finally know
The belief in the faith
That he did not show.

The cross should cause you to—
To do what?
What is it you need to do?

Joseph had a change of heart,
So can you.
Ask for Christ to come into your life.

He risked it all.
But for you, it's much simpler,
You just need to ask.

Christ will come in.
Christ will change your heart.
You risk nothing—you gain everything.

Just ask!

On the Third Day

Is your life a tomb,
Of dead men's bones?
Bones of your past,
Or is your life in CHRIST?

Die first then live second
Is not the way of earthly life.
The world says live for yourself,
Live first then die second.

To die first and live second
Is the way of life in CHRIST.
Die to self that you may live.
Death to self brings life?

Strange yet true.
You can die and remain
Or die and live,
HE gives that choice to you.

The stone that blocks true life
Is rolled away by HIM.
CHRIST wants you to enter in
And live anew.

Live by faith and belief.
Day 1 you die to self,
Day 2 you are in the tomb.
A tomb of leaving your past behind

Do you want to stay
Or do you want a 3rd day?
To arise, reborn
Into new life here and now.

The empty tomb changed HIS followers,
Does it change you?
Seek, ask, knock,
HE will arise new life in you.

Come out of your past
To remain is a tomb.
Leave the bindings of past behind.
Be wrapped in the light of HIS arising to new life.

On the Third Day 2

John 20:5–9

Napkin folded, set aside;
I AM not done,
I AM arisen
Means what to you.

I AM alive!
I can appear in your life
Because I died
And rose again.

IT IS FINISHED!
But something greater,
Something wondrous
Can begin in you.

I entered into death
For you.
I emerged from death
For you.

MY tomb is empty.
I entered new life
You can too
On your 3rd day.

A day of newness,
A day of renewal,
A day of arising,
A day of new life.

Look to ME.
Look to a new life together.
For I AM alive, anew,
For you.

Which One Are You?

Luke 23:33–43

One on the left,
One on the right.

One believed,
One did not.

One believed without seeing.
One saw and did not believe.

One had faith,
One did not.

That same day
Both entered eternity.

One entered paradise,
One entered condemned.

Believing is not something seen,
It is faith in the knowing.

One can look at the cross
And changes everything.

One on the left,
One on the right.

One was wrong,
One was not.

Which one are you?

The Road to Emmaus

LUKE *24:13–32*

How far along the road to Emmaus have you walked?
How far journey away, how lonely that walk?
How much hope lost, how blind your eyes?

Do you speak of it but not understand?
Do you despair of hopes not met?
When JESUS comes alongside, will you know it?

Men talking as they go, JESUS had died.
The man may be gone, but their SAVIOR lives,
Knowing not that CHRIST is alive, walking with them.

The world may veil your eyes to faith based on truth.
The truth of belief without seeing becomes inner sight.
Questions arise, but answers are found!

CHRIST is revealed to mind first, heart next,
SPIRITUAL eyes after that.
HE will reveal HIMSELF as you walk along.

On the road to Emmaus, JESUS showed HIMSELF,
Using the very word we hold today
In our hands, in our hearts.

Why didn't these two men write it all down?
No need, for it was already written
Even before it happened.

Do you want your heart to burn within
At the point where everything changes?
HE does not become alive, you do!

Next comes your personal book of Acts.
Done through you, by HIM
As you grow for HIM,

On the road to Emmaus, you discover that JESUS is alive.
You see you are no longer on the road alone,
HE comes alongside, HE becomes the way.

On My Way to You

On my way to YOU
I stumbled on the way.
On my way to YOU
I paused and caused delay.
On my way to YOU
I stopped to look at sin.
On my way to YOU
I doubted if YOU would let me in.
On my way to YOU
I often lost YOUR way.
On my way to YOU
I wasted many a day.
On my way to YOU
You approached me to say,
All you need do is follow
For I AM the way.
On my way to YOU
I often walked behind,
Wanting, trying to catch up
Wrestling within my mind.
On my way to YOU
You often turned to see,
Did he fall away or still following ME.
On my way to YOU
You often waited for me,
Urging me to continue
Never ceasing to beckon me.
On my way to YOU
I found mercy, love, forgiveness, grace.
On my way to YOU
I finally felt YOUR embrace.
On my way to YOU
At last I could see
The joy of a heaven
In simply knowing THEE.
On my way to YOU
The way is short or long
Depending on the things
I willfully drag along.
On my way to YOU
There is no journey end
For YOU always have
Greater joy just around the bend.

On my way to YOU
YOU enabled me to see
That all along
YOU were on your way to me.

Giving

Mark 12:41–44

She gave all she had,
Gave it all away.
Held nothing back
For another day.

Made no attempt to deceive,
Expected nothing in return.
Ending the day poorer
Than when it all began.

Poor in the world,
Yet rich in GOD!
Empty purse now
With heart so full.

She had needs
But GOD was greater.
Rather to keep for self,
To give away was better.

What became of her
The Word does not say.
But oh! how GOD must have rejoiced
On her final day!

The Little Things

Do you seek to do great things?
Start with things so little!
Little kind words,
A little prayer,
A little help,
All show you care.
All for free, every day,
For you to give away.

As you move through your day,
A little peace,
You can send on its way.
A little bit of heaven
Around you to create,
Indeed so small, and yet so great.
Little great things to be shown
Can bring a little heaven home.

The little things in life
Can become very great.
Start sharing now,
Never hesitate.
For some little thing
You do to another
Can earn for you
A new sister or brother.

3 Words

JOHN *19:28–30*

Tribulation, suffering, affliction.
Sin, pain, death.
FATHER, *forgive them!*

Do not fear.
You have victory.
I have overcome!

Forgiveness, mercy, grace.
Redemption, salvation, eternity.
It is finished!

This is Calvary.
I love you.
Come unto ME*!*

Put HIM first.
HIS will first.
HIS glory first.

Come HOLY SPIRIT.
Praise the LORD.
Thank you, GOD.

The 3 most powerful words
In all history.
"IT IS FINISHED!"

Never Forget

Special thanks to Pastor R. Bruschi II for his inspiration

Never forget
Is to always remember.
Always remember
Is to constantly think upon.

"I will never leave you or forsake you"
This is to say *I will never forget you,*
I will always think of you,
I will always remember
How special you are to ME.

Never forget.
Think upon those things.

Always remember
I left heaven for you,
Was born for you,
Lived for you,
Taught for you,
Healed for you,
Falsely accused for you,
Suffered and died for you,
Poured out MY *life for you,*
Arose for you,
Forgave you,
Gave you eternity.

I never forgot you,
Never forget ME.

"Whenever you eat or drink, do this in remembrance of ME*"*
This is MY *way of saying*
Never forget

Carried and Cast Away

Psalm 103:12 and Micah 7:19

You carried your sins,
The results are your burdens.
Guilt, remorse, regret.

When sins exposed,
Add more burdens.
Condemnation, reproach, shame.

Do not carry them
Inside heart and mind,
Do not allow the world to judge.

Carry them to ME
For I AM *the* JUDGE.
Let ME *carry your burdens.*

Let ME *carry them far away,*
"As far as the east is from the west,
Cast into the depths of the sea."

Carry forgiveness away with you,
Carry eternity away with you,
Carried by ME *to give to you.*

Drop the past you have carried.
Take up, carry MY *Cross,*
Follow ME.

I have taken you
And all that you carried,
Picked it all up, taken it from you.

Carried and cast away.

Watch with Me

Matthew 26:38

JESUS calls
To all of us.
Watch with ME
Stay with ME
Be with ME
Pray with ME.

Keep your eyes on ME,
Don't turn away.
Strive to see
What I see,
Long to feel
As I feel.

MY *garden*
Is your garden.
MY *death*
Is your life.
MY *resurrection*
Is your salvation.

MY *home in heaven*
Is also for you.
I AM *there*
To prepare A *place for you.*
It's waiting.

I AM *waiting*
For you,
I AM *calling*
For you,
I AM *watching*
For you,
To watch with ME.

Inside to Outward

Salvation comes down to man
And brings us up to GOD.
Touches us inside first,
Working from inside to out.

We work out our salvation,
That is to say,
HE gives it to us
To work it out in us.
To bring it forth,
To let it show.
New thoughts, new acts
Cause it to grow.

From the inner man
To the outer man
The heart and mind
Act upon the will.

A sinner, I
Receiving salvation
The gift of grace
Sufficient for my soul.

Ability given
To forgive, accept, love.
It all flows from
The inside out.

The Flow of Worship

Worship is a river,
Incessant it flows.
No obstacle impedes it,
Over, around everything it goes.

Worship is a river,
If temporarily dammed
It will fill the void
Until it bursts forth.

In the end
The river of worship always flows
Bearing you along.
Its course, only it knows.

The flow of worship
Will adjust your life,
Overcomes your circumstances,
Your obstacles, your strife.

Yield to worship
And its forever flow.
You begin with questions,
By the end, you will know.

Your own river of worship
Now rushing and bold,
Giving itself up
Flowing by streets of gold.

How Could?

How could they do this to me?
How could he, how could she?
How could a parent forget their child?
A spouse forget their mate?
How could someone forget
Their love for another?
How could they neglect, hurt, abuse
Those closest to their own lives?

When someone breaks the heart of another
Does it not also break the heart of GOD?

"Yes, it breaks MY heart—for I see that yours is broken.
I know this, for you are dear to ME,
I feel this, for I AM close to you.
I want you to be just as close to ME.

I can mend your broken heart
But it will take having MY presence in your life.
You can mend MY broken heart for you
By coming to ME,
Letting ME into your life
I know everything that has happened to you
But tell ME anyway.
Unburden the hurt, the pain, onto ME.

Go ahead and cry—first to yourself
Then cry to ME
MY understanding is there for you—always.
MY love is there for you—when you want it.
MY mercy is there for you—when you need it.
MY forgiveness is there for you—when you are ready for it,
Both for you and for those others.
Both to receive and to give
As you feel MY love, healing, restoration.

How can I do all this?
Because I came, lived, taught, died, and rose
For you, all that you are, all that you feel.
Now it is your turn to rise above.
How could you possibly do this?
With ME you can.
Begin by saying my name
"JESUS"

God Uses

God uses the naturally occurring things of this world
To accomplish the supernatural things of his kingdom.

Eternal love, his resurrected life was shown by death.

The light of eternal hope was given through temporary darkness.

Everlasting mercy was imparted by physical pain.

Unspoken truth was victorious over spoken lies.

Spiritual justice triumphed over men's deceitfulness.

His forgiveness erases our punishment.

Emotions dead come back to life.

Feelings broken become whole.

Hopes forgotten are fulfilled.

All of this is—
Love, mercy, grace, hope, forgiveness, truth, justice, salvation.

All of these are for you.
These are the things God uses.

I Need to See

I need to see myself
Different, better,
I need to see myself
The way GOD sees me.

The Word of GOD,
The gospel of CHRIST,
Helps me in this.
To see myself truer.

The clearer my sight,
The deeper the vision,
More of HIS will
Manifests in my life.

Nothing greater
Than HIS will,
Nothing greater
Than HIS sanctification.

More of HIS righteousness
For I have not my own.
More HIS love
Brings me to HIS throne.

More and more
Dead to sin.
More and more
Alive to HIM.

HIS mercy and grace
Renew my spirit
Now conformed
To HIS image.

HIS image
In me now,
This is what I need
To see.

Completely

GOD knows us completely.
Better than we know,
More than we know of
Ourselves.

Our hidden thoughts
Are not hidden to HIM.
Our hidden secrets
Are not secret to HIM.

Our failures
Are known to HIM.
Our hopes
Are known to HIM.

The more we know
Of ourselves, HE sees,
The more we see
What GOD sees.

Then maybe
We can catch
A glimpse
Of what HE wills for us.

HIS plan,
Our life,
HIS faithfulness
Becomes ours.

HIS Spirit
Awakens ours.
Now believing
We can give ourselves.

Completely.

Seeking Me

When you stop seeking ME
you lose sight of ME.
When you lose sight of ME
you create holes in your life.

Empty spaces
where I once dwelt.
Other things, worldly things
rush in to fill empty spaces.

They act as worldly patches
on spiritual holes.
A patch of ritual
where respect once was.
A patch of pride
where humble prayer once was.
A patch of anger
in place of love.

Overcome
As I have overcome.
I placed love
over everything.

Follow MY example.
Cover everything with love.
How?
Keep focused on this—
—keep seeking ME.

Holes in Your Garment

Our walk with the LORD is like a garment
you put on from time to time.
Times of closeness and intimacy,
times in the world and worldliness.

Remove your garment, look at it.
Hold it up to MY light.
Do you see rips and holes?
These are the empty spaces and hurts in your life.

Some holes the enemy has put there.
The holes of battles past.
Some holes you have put there.
Holes of indifference and disobedience.

A garment with holes lacks integrity,
does not protect the wearer.
Is not appealing to the wearer
or the onlooker.

You can take thread and sew.
You can take patches and mend.
*I would rather you leave that garment behind
and take* MINE.

Yes, take MY *garment, put it on.
I wore it specifically for you.
So that I could take it off
and give it to you.*

*Don't worry when you put holes in that one.
I will give you another and another,
and another, and another.
As many as it takes.*

*Until the day comes
when you will wear that final garment
the one of pure white
that one that will never get holes.*

Contradictions

We can soar to heights of SPIRIT
Fall to the depths of despair.

Face HIM in prayer
Turn away in sin.

Desire HIS presence
Hide in our sin.

Know with a certainty
Then doubt what we know.

Seeking forgiveness
Without repentance.

Life renewed
Without change.

Wanting the creation
Without the CREATOR.

Refusing truth
Believing lies.

Loving one
Despising another.

Wanting salvation
Without a SAVIOR.

Some contradictions will never fade
This is part of what man is—but not the last.
For salvation is dependent
On the ONE who saves.
HE in whom there is no contradiction.

You, Jesus

I was lost to myself,
You searched for me.
I was hidden in sin,
You found me.
I was in darkness,
You shone your light on me.

I was falling into hell,
You went ahead of me.
You caught me
Before I could land.
You rescued me
With love, grace, mercy, forgiveness.

You brought me up
Out of the darkness.
I could not walk,
You carried me.
You held me up
While I got to my feet.

You gave me a new way,
A new perspective,
A new life,
A new way to live.
In you,

Jesus.

Jesus 2

In your life
You taught us life.
You gave us forgiveness
So we could give forgiveness.

In your life
You changed water into wine,
Healed the sick,
Raised the dead.

To show our lives
Can be changed.
Sickness healed, addictions lifted
Lives become new again.

On the cross
You took on all darkness.
A world of sin
Including mine.

You cried out,
"my God, why have forsaken me?"
For a moment in time
Experienced separation from God.

So that I am free,
For all eternity
From separation from God.

For what you have done
Now it's my turn;
My life cries out,
Thank you.

It Is Not

It is not a burden
To carry the light of CHRIST
It is not a burden
To live for CHRIST
It is not a burden
To pray to CHRIST
It is not a burden
To show the love of CHRIST
It is not a burden
To trust in CHRIST
It is not a burden
To believe in CHRIST

It Is

It is a burden
To live in spiritual darkness
It is a burden
To live for nothing lasting
It is a burden
To face trials without prayer
It is a burden
To live without sharing love
It is a burden
To trust no one
It is a burden
To believe in nothing

GOD... Beyond... Whispers

GOD—beyond ancient,
Whispers—everlasting life.
We shall continue to exist
For there is no ceasing to be.
Do we rejoice?

Light shone on darkness
The light that lighteth every man.
It troubles our conscience,
Enlightens proofs of guilt,
Evidences of death—move us.

Between the upper millstone of hope
And the nether stone of fear
We are refined,
Made as dust.
Frightening.

But then—CHRIST!
Light through the gospel.
Divine life abolished death,
Divine death brought life.
Yea, even immortality.

GOD's eternity,
Man's mortality,
Join together.
Faith in CHRIST or eternal separation?
Choose!

Out of eternity—into time.
To rescue slaves of sin, of death.
From time to eternity,
GOD—beyond ancient,
Whispers—everlasting life.

The Price

Do you have the price
To obtain MY *grace,*
To receive MY *forgiveness?*
Do you have the price
Of righteousness
Or the cost of sanctification?

I know that you have it
Because I gave it to you.
Why don't you use it?
I have purchased these
For you
And more.

I can freely give
All this to you
Because the price
I paid in full
With MY *life,*
With MY *blood.*

Don't bury and hide
What I have given you,
What I have done for you.
The price I paid
So spend and use
Your talents wisely.

Obtain all that I have
Purchased for you.
The price?
It's free!

Alone?

Are you alone?
Forsaken?
Forgotten?

If you are alone
I can be with you.
I AM here,
In your heart

There is a place in your heart
For ME to dwell.
This is how our FATHER
Created you.

There is a place in MY heart
For you to dwell.
This is how it is
From the beginning.

You may feel you walk alone
But you only need to ask ME;
I will come alongside.

You may feel alone
But seek ME;
I AM always there.

With ME, you are never forgotten
With ME, you are never forsaken
With ME, you are never alone.

Was, Are, I Am

there was once people in your life
who are now gone

there are people in your life
who may not always be there for you

let ME be there for you
always in all ways
in your life, heart, and mind
in your body, spirt, and soul

there is no void
that I cannot pervade
there is no emptiness
that I cannot fill

I AM not offering you a substitute
I AM offering something different
hard to explain

you will know it
when you feel it

MY something is unmistakable

it goes from secret to open
hidden to revealed
yet, at the same time
from without to within

there was
there are
people in your life
I AM ONE of them

Heaven's Shore

The souls of those
Who journey away,
Whom during life were sure
Of God's deep sea of love,
Sail to heaven's distant shore.

To our hearts, it seems unwise
That they should leave us so.
For their ship of soul departs
From our port of grief,
So hard to let them go.

And yet, their sailing
Is so much smoother
Than we who remain can see.
For they dock in heaven's harbor
Anchored at peace eternally.

We mourn the sailing away of love,
The love we got,
The love we gave.
It seems so unreal to us,
So the memories we save.

In this time of sailing away
It is a blessing to know
That their new life in heaven
Is so much greater
Than that which came before.
For they have sailed from here
To land on heaven's shore.

Just You and Me

GOD holds you
Whatever befalls.
HE comes close,
HE knows your heart calls.

HE knows your thoughts,
HE feels your tears.
Which look ahead
With anxieties, fears.

HE gives strength needed
For the longing within.
HE already witnessed
Your days of sorrow.
HE already ordained
There will be tomorrow.

Times of remembrances,
Thoughts rise and fall.
Seeming to surround you
HE helps bear them all.

For in HIS arms
Which you cannot see
HE takes you up
Whispers, *"Just you and Me."*

*"I love you so much,
I shrink from your pain
For I bear it with you
Over and over again.*

*But with my love
Comes life anew,
For in your heart;
Always me, always with you!"*

Sometimes

Sometimes I walk ahead of you,
Wanting you to follow.

Sometimes I walk behind you,
Urging you forward.

Sometimes I walk alongside you
In fellowship you and I.

Those times spent alongside,
I like those times better!

I can turn and see your face,
You can turn and see MINE.

Sometimes walking together,
Silently touching each other's presence.

Holding your hand
As you hold MINE.

Those are the best times,
Which are really up to you.

I AM *always there for you,*
So sometimes can become always.

Here I Am

Jesus *says, "Here* I am."
Some spend their lives seeking
Book after book,
Conference after conference,
Meeting after meeting,
Church after church,
Hoping to find ME.
Some travel the world,
Thinking I can be found
After running around.

Here I am,
I have been right here
Waiting for you.
You have chased ME
But never turned to ME.
Studied ME
But never accepted ME.
Wanted MY *presence*
But not partake of MY *life.*
When your studies are finished
And the wandering done,
You must return home,
To yourself.

Here I am
Waiting for you
From the beginning.
After you come through amazement
As when I called Philip,
Who instantly believed
For I saw him under a tree.
After you come through questioning
As John's disciples,
Are YOU *the* CHRIST?
After you come through denying
As Peter denied,
Only to proclaim love for ME *again.*
After you come through doubting
As Thomas,
Unless I see I will not believe.
After all this.

Here I AM.
I will come to you.
I will reveal MY *presence*
Through MY SPIRIT,
We will touch each other's heart.
MY *message is simple.*
Do you want to find ME?
Here I AM!

Never

I have never traveled the world
Yet I have beheld the wonder of creation.

I have never been to the stars beyond my sight
Yet I know that they are there.

I have no outward riches coveted by man
Yet I have hidden riches untold within.

I have no palace for an earthly home
Yet I have a mansion awaiting in heaven.

I have never stood before royalty
Yet I have bowed before the KING OF KINGS.

I have never seen my LORD
Yet I am blessed by not seeing and believing.

I may have most of my life behind me
Yet I have eternity ahead.

Never Let

Never let
The life of CHRIST
In you
To divide

Never let
Oneness
Become two

Never let
Spiritual growth
Stagnate

Never let
Hate replace love
Fear replace hope

Never let
Trials
Drive you away
From ME

Always Allow

Always allow
My life
To merge
With yours

Always allow
Two become one
You and ME

Always allow
My Spirit
To grow yours

Always allow
My love and hope
Become real to you

Always allow
Trials of life
Bring you
To ME

Salvation

GOD and sin merged.
The result,
The cross of CHRIST.
Salvation.

GOD's judgment of sin.
The cross
Not a punishment,
The cross is victory.

Time and eternity met.
A gateway opened
To redemptive relationship.
Salvation.

The cross did not come into the life of JESUS.
JESUS came putting HIS life into the cross.
Salvation.

Now we can come
Partake of that life,
Partake of salvation.

Incarnation accomplished redemption.
The redemption is salvation.
A moment in time and yet eternal,
A physical event in the realm of Spirit.

For those who are saved
The cross raises no questions
Yet provides all the answers.

GOD's nature revealed
HIS love for us
Opened eternity.
Salvation from sin.

The Cross

The cross is HIS judgment of my sin,
The sin HE sees in me.

HIS cross is punishment for my sin,
The punishment HE took for me.

The cross is HIS salvation from my sin,
The salvation HE gave to me.

Through the cross, I find
Righteous judgment,
Heaven's eternal gate,
Open and calling to me.

The cross shows both
My sin and salvation,
My judgment and acquittal.
Punishment canceled; freedom given.

The cross is a crossroad.
Denial leads to separation,
Acceptance leads to heaven.
They meet at the intersection of choice.

The cross is the summation
Of my life before CHRIST.
Nothing can criticize me, judge me,
More than the cross.

But here is the *good news*,
That is not the purpose of the cross.
The cross is hope,
The cross is new life arisen.

Bring Me through the Cross

I've seen the cross distant in my life,
I've seen the cross come closer to me,
I've seen the cross beckon to me.
Incomprehensible to reconcile.

I've seen the cross become clearer.
As I come to the cross,
LORD, take me further,
Take me through the cross.

Take me past the symbol,
Take me into the truth.
Bring me through the cross,
Bring me closer to YOU.

That I may see the cross,
Beyond which
Is the living CHRIST.
The cross now understood.

Now living for CHRIST
Brings me through the cross
Into HIS presence,
HIS presence is life anew.

Life sure and true
For the cross in the past,
My future in YOU.
For the cross is a journey.

The start, the beginning, the door,
The goal of which is through the cross,
The goal is the life of CHRIST.
Eternal life secure.

The cross is but a part
So I go through the cross
To CHRIST HIMSELF.
Bring me through the cross.

Fallow Ground

Not turned
Not planted
No growth
No fruit
Life untouched
Empty

Once seeded
Unchanged becomes changed
Fallow becomes fruitful
Dark become light
Ungodly becomes godly
Unredeemed becomes redeemed

Thoughts
Emotions
Actions
Habits
Go from untouched
To touched by GOD

Fallow ground
Awaiting seed
Longing to be cultivated
Bearing harvest
All of us
And you

Through It All

Sadness in my life,
Through it all
There is YOU.

Loss in my life,
Through it all
There is YOU.

Pain in my life,
Through it all
There is YOU.

Overcoming all
Is there,
Because of YOU.

Joy in my life
Is there,
Because of YOU.

Release in my life
Is there,
Because of YOU.

Freedom in my life
Is there,
Because of YOU.

All of life,
Beginning to end.
Through it all,
Because of YOU.

I Walked Away

I walked away,
You followed me.

I ran away,
You chased me.

I hid from YOU,
You looked for me.

I denied YOU,
You affirmed me.

I rejected YOU,
You accepted me.

I nailed YOU to a cross,
You took it willingly.

You died,
So I could live.

You arose,
That I may rise up.

That one day,
Together,
We can walk away.

Know This

Jesus walks alongside,
His footprints unseen.

Jesus places his hand in ours.
We do not feel its warmth.

Jesus speaks to us,
But only our hearts hear.

The love of Jesus,
Always present.

Yet we ignore it,
Give it no thought.

But know this,
He walks unseen,
Touches unfelt,
Speaks in silence.

Know this.
He is real.
As alive as you and I.

If You—I Am

If you come to ME
With the hope of expectation,
I will come to you
With the joy of fulfillment

If you sing praises to ME
Coming from your heart,
I will sing blessings upon you
From MY *abundance of love.*

If you will pray to ME
When with others,
I will pray for you
When before our FATHER.

If you work for ME
In ways that I can see,
I will work for you
In ways you cannot see.

If you are waiting for ME,
No need to wait any longer.
I AM *right here, right now,*
With you always in all ways.

If you seek a life renewed,
I will give that to you.
If you seek salvation from sin,
I AM *that salvation.*

If you come to ME,
You will discover
Something true and wonderful,
I AM!

Trees and Mountains

Luke 17:6 and Mark 11:23

Mountains of despair
Mountains of hurt
Mountains of loss
Mountains of regret.

Have faith
That starts out small.
As small as a mustard seed
The smallest of seeds.

Plant it, feed it, nurture it.
Allow your faith to grow into a tree
The tree destiny calls you to be
With a faith firm and true.

Now with faith strong
You can say to those mountains
That you cannot overcome,
Be removed and cast into the sea.

The sea of HIS love
Covers mountains vast,
Cast away to the sea
Mountains of your past.

Now HE calls you
To walk on the water
Away from your mountains.
Come rest in the shade
Of the tree of HIS faith.

It Is Enough

What do I have to look forward to?
I have JESUS in my life!
It is enough.

JESUS will not take control until I give it to HIM,
And when HE does,
It is enough.

I have in HIM, life in HIM.
This in and of itself is sufficient,
It is enough.

JESUS is willing to become my sin.
To cover it, to forgive it,
It is enough.

Is HE not then as willing to cover my life
With HIS presence?
It is enough.

HE is bigger, better than everything
I have been chasing.
HE is the KING of my heart.

Is it enough?
It is more than enough!

But—

Happiness is externally based,
It comes from the outside in
But—
Joy is internally cherished,
It comes from the inside out.

Goodness is showing outward behavior
But—
Righteousness is living the promise.

Coming to is a process
But—
Abiding with is the process completed.

Believing is proving to oneself
But—
Knowing is absolute assurance.

Obedience is improvement striving
But—
Intimacy is closeness accomplished.

Go

Meet life and trials
With faith in HIM.
Reflecting like a mirror,
Your faith made stronger.

Strife and trials fade,
Sight and sound give way
To an eternal ocean,
Reflecting eternal lights.

Faith rises again,
A song of victory.
Old life in retrospect,
New life of prospect.

In a distant place called
With HIM forever.
First come to HIM
Then go on with HIM.

To a heavenly realm
Called faith.
Go!

"Follow Me"

Follow ME *is the answer to life's problems,*
Is the beginning of true joy.
Follow ME *has a promise attached,*
It is a struggle with happiness.
Follow ME *has responsibilities to bear,*
Of obedience, of repentance, of change.
Follow ME *has blessings,*
Of forgiveness, of renewal.
Follow ME *is not judgment,*
But acceptance.
Follow ME *means self-denial,*
Leading to self-fulfillment.
Follow ME *is your life's purpose,*
Life's goal, the way, the truth.
Follow ME *is the salvation,*
Of eternal life.
Follow ME *means that I invite you,*
To be present, intimate with ME.
Follow ME *is not a life patch,*
It is teaching you new life.
Follow ME *pierces your body,*
Reaches past your ego,
Touches your soul,
Lifts your spirit.
Follow ME,
For I AM *alive today.*

Touching Your Heart

If I were to touch your heart
Would you feel MY presence?

If I were to speak to you
Would you know MY voice?

If I were to walk alongside you
Would you want to walk on alone?

If I were to take your hand
Would you pull it away?

If you give ME your heart
I could speak to you,
I could touch you,
I could walk with you,
I could hold you close.

You would without doubt
Hear when I speak,
Feel when I touch,
Sense MY presence,
Know I take your hand.

All these things I do and more.
For these are the beginning
Of being together, you and I.
From here we rise up
To greater, truer, higher things.

If you would only let ME start
By touching your heart.

Water and Fire

My HOLY SPIRIT *is described as both a river and a fire.*
It flows as a river and washes away only the bad,
The good is left standing, clean and refreshed.
When it burns as a fire, it is all consuming,
The good is left standing, finer and stronger.

Only in ME
Can SPIRIT's *water and* SPIRIT's *fire coexist.*
Only in ME
SPIRIT's FIRE *is not extinguished by* SPIRIT's *water.*

When MY HOLY *river flows,*
It will never put out MY HOLY *fire.*
The flow will cause fire to grow stronger, brighter,
For you, in you.

MY *water and* MY *fire work together,*
For your spirit, your life, your well-being.
The fire burning is the release,
The river flowing is the result.

The fire burns down the wall
That held back the river.
Let the fire of MY SPIRIT *burn down your walls.*
Walls of your past, your regrets, your hurts.

MY HOLY SPIRIT's *water, nothing impedes,*
It flows incessantly.
MY HOLY SPIRIT's *fire burns forever.*
Let MY *water and fire come into your life.*

Am I?

am I stubborn or submitted
spoiled or giving
carnal or spiritual
irritable or peaceful
begrudging or forgiving
cynical or sincere
pretending to or praying for

am I set on my way or yielded
self-aware or identified with CHRIST

am I in two worlds
living in one and wanting the other
tolerating one to glimpse the other
surrendering one to grasp the other

I am!

I am two natures
two creations
encompassed in duality
opposites that touch
physical with spiritual
death clothed with eternity
perfectly created imperfection
emptiness seeking fulfillment
ignorance longing wisdom
I am two
longing to be one

I Am a Psalm

To become a song
Not of myself.

A song for others
Sung in awe of GOD.

A song brought forth
By the unheard voice.

A song as anointing oil
Soft, fragrant, sweet.

A song that sings
Of HIS mystery, majesty.

Faithfulness, love, forgiveness, authority,
Unending eternal lyrics.

A song as leaves in the breeze.
A singing bird is creation's song.

Creation's songs show mysteries hidden.
Man is also a song hidden.

Awaiting to be sung,
By each to everyone.

One's life to become a song,
A psalm of HIS singing.

We are a song of GOD
Bring it forth, know it, sing it.

I carry in my heart a song.
My soul sings out.

I am a psalm of GOD.

Gratitude

GOD's gifts to you
If taken one by one,
As they come,
Awakens your gratitude.

Gratitude should lead you to thanksgiving.
Gratitude should lead you to praise.
Gratitude should lead you to worship.
Gratitude should lift your spirit.

From the smallest of GOD's gifts
To the largest of GOD's gifts,
Each gift
Each a miracle.

When GOD's hands are upon you,
HIS mind was upon you first.
Even HIS thoughts of you
Are a miracle.

When gifts from GOD
Fall upon you,
Praise and thanks
Lifted up be your reply.

It is often said
GOD speaks through HIS word,
GOD speaks through HIS servants,
GOD speaks through HIS creation.

It is also divine truth
GOD speaks through HIS blessings.
Blessing which bring forth in you,
Gratitude.

Communion—Next Time

Next time you take communion
That is, say the bread or wafer
Upon your tongue
Leave it there.

Don't chew it
Don't sallow it
Just leave it there
Let it dissolve.

Concentrate your thoughts
Turn and focus senses
On this morsel
Upon your tongue.

Let it take over
Your feelings
Your thoughts
Your concentration.

This is how it should be
With CHRIST
All the time
"I AM *the bread of life*."

On our mind
In our heart
In our mouths
All the time.

For a brief moment
This experiment
Simple and small
Becomes powerful.

A powerful sign
Of a relationship
Real and lasting
Effect on our life.

It can begin
The next time
With you and HIM
In communion.

He Is

He is a rock
When I am sand.

He is nearby
To take my hand.

He is a mighty flood
When I am rain.

His flood of love
Covers my pain.

He is the light of day
In my darkest hour.

A blossom of strength
Showing his power.

He lifts me up
When I am down.

He shows that hope
In him is found.

Mighty, stronger, surer, safer
He is my Lord,
Christ the Savior.

Fulfilled 1

JESUS fulfilled the purpose of HIS life.
Accomplished the will of the FATHER.
Knew why HE came.
Knew HE must suffer, die, arise.

I do not know the end as JESUS knows.
I do not know HIS plan.
If not able to know,
Cause me to rest, knowing I am being led.

Led to live YOUR will,
To make my life fulfilled.

Fulfilled 2

*I was obedient unto death,
So I can ask you to be obedient in little things.
I suffered without saying a word,
So you can suffer to less a degree,
A mere fraction of a fraction.*

*I died for your sins.
This is our FATHER's will
For your life.
In MY death are many lessons on life
Beyond the lesson of dying for your sins.
Dying for your sins brings you new life.*

*I poured out MY life for you,
That I could pour it into you.
Now you can pour into the lives of others.
I have wounds great and immeasurable.
MY wounds heal your smaller ones
And give you life fulfilled.*

Here I Am

Here I am in my creation.
Here I am for my people.
Here I am to teach my ways.
Here I am to give my healing.
Here I am to give my mercy and grace.
Here I am to give my forgiveness.
Here I am to die
For all your sins.
Here I am to rise
For your salvation.
Here I am for your eternity
For I already have mine,
So I came for yours.

Choose

You die with your sin,
Eternal separation.
Or through ME, sin dies in you,
Eternal salvation.
Your sin not covered up,
Your sin not suppressed,
But your sin crucified with ME.
Your sin lives, you die.
Your sin dies, you live.
Choose.

If Only

If only able to grasp THY hand
My fears would turn to strength.
If only able to behold THY face
My doubt would surely die.
If only able to understand THY will
Would cause me joyful surrender.
If only able to glimpse THY boundless love
Then there could be no words,
Only a feeling incomprehensible.
Oh! If only.

Embark

I am about to embark on a journey, with me you cannot come.
I may travel for years, yet I am never leaving home.
I will be gone awhile, but I shall never leave you alone.

Some have traveled already, signs unseen show the way,
To a path I see with my heart, as I look past darkness to day.

At times, nowhere it leads, and I wonder why I went,
Other times, it floods with light, all effort made well spent.

This way is often rough, sometimes I catch a breeze,
And feel I can walk forever, and never get off my knees.

I hear a call, not with my ears.
Conscious yet unknowing, is the journey over or is this path growing?

As the path disappears behind, I move forward even faster,
Finding I walk alone, with an invisible MASTER.

HE takes me home again, to a home I never saw,
As if I just revisited, a home never seen before.

I stand before myself, not to recognize who I see,
For the man who began this journey is no longer me.

I find myself in two worlds, in love with the bride and the groom.
Within this home wherein I dwell, there is an unlocked room.

In this room, there is a throne, on which I never sit,
But I can come whenever I like, to rest from the world a bit.

The journey is at its end, but it never will be over.
Even when in the ground I lay, HE will come and tap my shoulder.

Then the journey starts anew, much easier than before,
For now I know where I am going, I have visited that distant shore.

The Road

Dedicated and with grateful thanks to Senior Pastor R. Bruschi,
Founder of Freedom Road Bible Church

On the road to glory, as a solider I must stay.
On the road to glory are checkpoints along the way.

The battle begins with surrender, for you give all you are.
The first checkpoint is submission to a power near but far.

The next checkpoint is obedience, to the Word which was given.
Followed closely by perseverance, you are faithful, committed, driven.

The final checkpoints include service and servanthood,
As a solider, you give because you want, not because you should.

On this road to glory, the enemy will always attack
But the only thing to fear is your turning back.

You are on the road to glory, blind to all but the goal
For ahead, there is a cross at the end of this road.

You do not reach it for yourself
You come there only for HIM.
You finish with surrender again
The same way you did begin.

Scared from battle and full of light
The last checkpoint appears,
To willingly lay down and die
With joy shinning in your tears.

The Cross Wasn't There!

To Mary Lyons, founder of Mount Holyoke Women's Seminary

Huge, imposing, made of stone
Solid wood surrounds an empty throne
Ivy covered, topped by clouds
Granite, marble, nothing surrounds

As I drew near
The bigger it grew
A feeling of mind
Into heart withdrew

The pews are there
Dimly lit
So none can see
A pulpit to un-divinity

Candles unlit
Old still new
Honor given
To whom?

Books of hymns
Mouthed not sung
For in this temple
Dwells no one

I entered with reverence
Walked down the marble road
Such a great structure
Stood all alone

Out of awe, I sang a song
A mighty fortress is our GOD
To HIS ears only
Did it belong

The more my heart moved
To the inner place
Eyes realized a sorrow
Disgrace

The cross wasn't there
The cross wasn't there

Up white stairs
Hung scarlet majesty
Multicolored circle of light
An empty expanse met my sight

The cross wasn't there
What had happened, why?
Is HE no longer correct?
Has another way been found?

Another lie been told
From another serpent on the ground
In the silence, my heart shouts out
JESUS! Why did they take YOUR cross out?

All the grandeur
Of this once holy place
Is brought to naught
A holy disgrace

In tear-filled eyes I see
An empty edifice
To honor nothing
Because the cross wasn't there

My GOD, my GOD
Why have we forsaken YOU?

Not just a church
Now become a great hall
It stands for all the faith lost, surrendered
Given up to new trustfulness

Sob echoed in empty splendor

For a brief moment
HE came back smiling
HE was there still
For I carry HIM in my heart

I can invoke HIS holy presence
By my love alone

Discipleship Is

Brokenness

Repentance

Humility

Servanthood

Loving-kindness

Righteousness

Self-discipline

Study

Openness

Willingness

Closeness

Intimacy

Forsaking

Accepting

Manifesting

Words

Jesus
Became
Man
Begotten
Unique
Moral
Sinless
Perfect
Teacher
Love
Compassion
Mercy
Truth
Grace
Miracles
Healing
Seek
Save
Lost
Nailed
Atoned
Died
Sins
Intercession
Salvation
Completed
Arose
Alive
Today
Forever
You

The Desire

Heed the desire
Of your searching heart.
The heart that is seeking
For peace.

Search and see
JESUS appears
In emotion.
Invisible longing.

Our spirit awakes
To a mental vision.
Your life renews
By HIS SPIRIT.

Peace is given
But then,
It all returns.
The commonplace.

The everyday,
Duties,
People,
Mistakes made.

You smother
Until you heed the desire
Of your searching heart.
Search for JESUS.

The Call to Worship.

I have called you to worship;
But not as you may think.

Worship of ME
Is not only something
You do in church
With music and singing.

Worship ME *in your relationships.*
Worship ME *in your home.*
Worship ME *at work.*
Worship ME *at play.*

Worship ME *by your words,*
Your actions, your deeds.

Worship of ME
Is a never-ending circle.
Starts with you, reaches ME,
Touches you, constantly moving.

Worship of ME
Honors ME,
All that I stand for
In all that you do.

This is what I call worship.

Love Is More

Love is more than dreams,
More than dreams fulfilled.

Love is more than hope,
It goes beyond that goal.

Love goes past sharing,
Entering realms of unity.

Love is not two,
Not even one,
One can be divided.

Love leaves surrender behind,
Becoming willing sacrifice.

Love is not waiting for,
But abiding with.

Love is not me,
Love is not you,
Love is us, together.

GOD has not only love for us,
GOD is the love we have.

Each other,
With HIM,
Just the three of us.

Become one.

CHOICES

Standing on a cliff of choices
Gazing into time's vast expanse
Past, present, future before you
Time and space met in one place
This time, this here, this now, this you

Look up and see a shining citadel coming on the clouds
Or look down into a valley of dry bones
The unwanted relative of the past is regret
The present has longing as its children
The future has hope like a cherished love

Choices made can seem like dreams
That never really arrive
For you awake back in the present
You choose for dream's vision
But often find a mirror that reflects emptiness

Choices made can become real dreams
Brought into reality by belief
To awaken your future hope
You chose to strive for dream's vision
And find the mirror that reflects inner light

To question why, maybe cry, even ponder how
A question without answer yet
My mind can grasp and accept for now
Store it away and faithfully wait
Someday, the answer will come

To question why, maybe cry, even ponder how
Can an answer be given without a question?
The answer has the question hidden within it
Sometimes, the answer comes first, store it away
Understanding will be shown, by faith it will come

Standing on a cliff of choices
Do we jump down or arise above?
Climb higher to the next cliff, the next choice
More than just a crossroad
A precipice of decision before us

Turn away from the cliff or stay and pray
It is either back down the way you came
Or up, beyond the precipice
Above this cliff to one higher yet
The true choice always inside us, put there by HIM

YOURS

LORD, may my heart be as YOURS
my soul sing to YOURS
my thoughts be as YOURS
my ways become YOURS
my life reflect YOURS
my life hidden in YOURS

call me YOUR child
call me YOUR servant
so in this life
all that I am
all that I do
is YOURS

Merry Christmas

We give our cares to HIM
But do we give our hearts?
We lift up our burdens to HIM
But do we lift up our spirits?

We send our prayers to HIM
But do we send our praises?
We silently voice our discontents
But do we audibly give our thanks?

The world would have us say
Season's greetings
Have a great holiday
But not Merry Christmas!

The world will sing of
Happy holidays
And silver bells
But not sing of the great love of HIS freely given salvation.

We will "Deck the Halls"
Travel "Over the River and Through the Woods"
And go "Home for the Holidays"
But not set aside a time just for HIM.

CHRIST does not live in our hearts but one day a year
But all the days of the year.
Therefore, I will keep CHRIST in Christmas
Whatever the world may think matters not.

As for me and my house
We will say
Merry Christmas!

3:00 a.m.

God likes three o'clock in the morning.
He can speak to me then.

I am asleep, quiet, and still.
I am empty and receptive.

No thoughts about the day past.
No thoughts about the day ahead.

There are no distractions of creation,
No noise of the world.

He can wake me and speak to me.
If receptive I can hear.

Hear his leading,
Put down on paper.

Hopefully live by it.
Share it through my life.

God likes three o'clock in the morning.

Yourself

Earthly thoughts, earthly needs
Show you things
Not always HIS will.

Lacking perception of HIS power,
His love, HIS grace, HIS forgiveness
Is sonship not realized.

Blessings not yet known,
Not yet proven to yourself
Holds you back.

Consent and accept the blessings.
Trials become lessons,
Burdens become light.

Now you become HIS
As fear becomes courage,
Weakness becomes strength.

Now with new thoughts, new needs,
Comes willful consent to offer HIM
Your will to HIS.

Yourself to HIM.

Show Me

You show me
My faults
My mistakes
My sins
By
Your mercy
Your grace
Your forgiveness

You give me
My redemption
My freedom
My salvation
By
Your love
Your cross
Your sacrifice

Accept my submission
To your authority

Let my life
Become your will

Your home in heaven
Becomes mine

Your eternity
Becomes my eternity

When I become yours
All this
You show me

In Your Life

GOD comes into your life
The way HE wants,
Not necessarily the way you want.

JESUS went to prepare a place for you.
Should you prepare a place for HIM?
A place in mind, heart, soul.

GOD made room for you in HIS life,
Make room for HIM in yours.
Accept FATHER, SON, SPIRIT.

Anticipate HIM,
Look for HIM,
Want HIM.

HE not only comes when HE wants,
But it will not take HIM long,
To do what HE wants,
Which is the best for you.

By whatever means HE chooses,
HE may even surprise you.
For all of a sudden, HE is there.

Unexpected, unannounced
HE shows up
In your life.

For what HE wants
Is to be right now
In your life.

See Me

You cannot see ME standing here
But standing, here I AM
Right now, beside you.

You cannot see ME standing here
With your eyes, I know
Within you is a special sight
An insight that can grow.

In you is that which can see ME
I put it there for you
For when you find it
It in turn finds you.

Inner eyes with inner vision
Inner eyes that seek
Inner eyes that desire
Dare to take a peek.

To see ME as I AM
To catch a glimpse of ME
To see things invisible
Like love, vast and free.

At that time
When at last you can see
We move on to hearing
(and please excuse the pun)
Can you hear ME now?

All I have for you to hear
Will partner with your sight
For when you see ME
Former darkness becomes light.

Now you can know ME
Now you can hear ME
Now you can see ME.

I Am Standing Right Here

Are you there, God?
Are you the king?
Are you the Lord over everything?
I need you now!

Are you real?
Do you love me?
The world's tearing me down,
My soul can't breathe.
Can I see you now?

"Why do you say you can't see me?
My love for you is real.
Waiting to enter your life
In my unique ways.
Be sure of my love.
Draw closer to me.

Why can't you see,
I'm always near.
If you could want what I want,
All awaiting right here!
But where are you now?
Come to me now!
I'm waiting right here.

I am your God
I am your king
I came and died
That you may have everything.
Where am I now?
I'll tell you right now,
I am standing right here!"

Lord, I Trust You

Lord, to you I trust my life,
To you I trust my love.
I trust in your will,
Given from heaven above.

I trust in your leading,
Guiding all my years.
I trust in your calming
All of my fears.
I trust in your cherishing
All of my tears.
I trust in your healing
All of life's pains.
I trust in your light
After life's rains.

I trust in your salvation
Of my eternal soul.
I trust in your Spirit
That leads me to know
That all this written above
Is how you show your love.

Because your love
Leads to all the rest,
Lord, I trust you,
Are words that seem best.

For Family

The Tree of JESUS

For Donna—my life, my strong tree

There is a seed from a tree called the love of JESUS.
HE plants this seed in your heart.
Water this seed with HIS Word,
It will grow and never depart.

As the seed puts out roots, as seeds always do,
Roots that are never seen,
A work begins inside of you.
Visible growth unseen.

As the roots grows, so does the tree,
Firm, unmovable, strong.
The tree now a living word,
Others may come, rest in the shade.

From a seed grows a tree called the love of JESUS,
Always bears fruit in due season.
Your arms become love's branches with fruit so sweet.
Fruit of HIS life in you made complete.

When the winds of strife cause your life to waver,
Your faith gets tested, run to your SAVIOR.
HE is waiting for you, arms open wide,
That's how HE lived, that's how HE died.

Yes, HE is waiting for you under HIS tree,
The unmovable place of joy and safety.

Where is HIS tree?
I hope you remember,
It is inside your heart,
And will live there forever.

For Faith, for Life

To urge your ship to leave port
Where waters move slow
You must strain at the oars for a while
Face the past as you row

Once set free
From the past you see
Set course for the open sea
Where new ports await thee

What happens, o ship, when docks fade
And you strive toward open sea
Find as you leave the past behind
You row more easily

When gentle winds begin to stir
You feel them touch your face
Set sail to catch the breeze
Set course to a distant place

Open doors long shut
Open portholes, hatches
Invite the fresh breeze inside
If need be, break rusty latches

Now that your sails are spread
You lay your oars aside
They rest, no longer needed
To the ship's rudder you stride

As the pilot of your ship
You stand and face the bow
Gage the wind, set a course
Higher goals upon your brow

Keep watch for rocks and shallows
Waves crash against your hull
Off course they try to move you
Into death like sleep they lull

If you dock in ports unwanted
And wonder how here you came
Pull up your anchor, set sail again

Return to MY sea, always the same

O sailor, you cannot move your ship
That is done by wind and tide
You may believe you direct it
But a star is truly your guide

You begin to enter new waters
Clearer than the rest
Your rudder surrenders to another
For an inward course is set

For to spread your sails
Is to come before GOD
You do this by simple prayer
Then the wind of MY SPIRIT shall move you
And MY presence will find you there

Beloved sailor, ready your ship
Set sails and come unto ME
I AM vast, always flowing
The eternally present sea

Your goal is MY distant shore
Upon the journey's end
From the ship you disembark
For life here does not depend
On ships and oars or even sails
But only upon MY grace
Which now you see never fails
I know by the look on your face.

The Eyes of Lazarus

For Mike, for life

Lazarus lay in his grave
Although soul eternally saved
As he lies in the dark
Soul still has life, spark

As he lies there
What do his eyes see
Does he see those times
He walked with eternity

Does he see the time
Spent at HIS feet
As he sees backward
Is his life complete

Does he see the face
Recall the time spent
In the presence of his MASTER
From heaven sent

Does he see the healing
The love, the tears
Does he see the courage
To conquer all fears

Then the soul hears that command
Larazus, come forth!

Out of dark death
To the light of life
Lazarus emerges
Then his eyes reopened

What did Lazarus see
A world shrouded in wrappings
Then wrappings of death are removed
The light of the world reenters his soul

Now look at the world
Through Lazarus's eyes
The sun must have been brighter
Then he ever realized

Lazarus resees creation
With eyes renewed
Because his LORD
Commanded him to

His eyes regain sight
Sight becomes vision
Vision has become hope
Hope is held in the soul

Lazarus sees more now
Then he has ever seen before
The eyes of his soul
Thirst, hunger for more

Lazarus sees beyond his eyes
He sees with mind, sees with his heart
He again sees his LORD
From whom he will never depart

It's most important
That you should know
Is that Lazarus can now see
With his soul

As you walk through life
Your journey will grow
So see with the eyes
That come from your soul

See with the eyes of Lazarus

Mary's Smile, Laura's Smile

For Laura Grace

To Mary, many gifts did GOD impart—

I believe Laura has Mary's smile
For it lights up an entire room
I believe Laura has Mary's laughter
For it chases away darkness and gloom
I believe Laura has Mary's love
For it shows, though hidden in her heart
I believe Laura has Mary's grace
It lies in her nature, shines through her face

Mary's smile must have been deep and wide
To express all the love held inside
Mary's laughter must have been free and sweet
As a song sung with love complete
Mary's love must have been trusting
Her grace as a vessel overflowing

My little Laura Grace has all this and more
My prayers are that these grow as she grows
Today and evermore

For as you grow, my Laura Grace
Remember the simple gifts given
Such as a smile and laughter
They can be a gift to others
As well as a gift to your own soul

Remember the harder gifts
Of love and grace
And never let anything else
In your heart take their place

So much love through Mary came
That the world was changed
Was never the same

Do you have that power to alter a life?
I believe that you do
For I have seen it in your smile

His Name Is John

Bible in hand, quiet time, reflecting, half awake, half asleep.
Suddenly a voice! Audible? Or in my head?
"His name is John!"

Suddenly wide awake, senses ablaze.
What was that, looking around,
Did someone say something, what was that sound?

"His name is John!"
In my head won't go away.
What am I to do, what am I to say?

Yes, LORD, his name will be John.
In the SPIRIT of that messenger, I hope he will grow,
Others to lead, others to show.

Like that messenger, a simple life.
Awaiting his LORD, awaiting new life.

To know without testing, trial, or doubt
To accept HIS heart, then let HIM out.

To stand on the side, telling the story
So that ONE greater can get all the glory.

To willingly cease, to humbly decrease
That HIS ministry only increase.

Proud parents, Elizabeth and Zechariah
To see their son John proclaim the MESSIAH.

Proud parents we, for what could be better,
Than to see our John know his SAVIOR.

The LORD declares,
"His name is John, once yours, always MINE!"

My Son John

You don't know how hard it was
To keep a smile on my goodbye.
You didn't see a father's heart, break down and cry.

You have no concept of my worry and fear,
My desire to keep you near.
All you see is, your journey is here.

I know that youth and adventure call.
Your time at hand to stand or fall.
All I can do is pray as you go.

New life before you that doesn't include mine.
I let you go willingly and unwillingly
At the same time.

Go! Experience, grow, explore,
I know you shall return
Stronger than before.

From HIS hands you came,
Into HIS hands you go.
HIS choice, this I know.

So study and learn
The lessons of life.
Including joys, sometimes strife.

Stand on your own with HIM at your side.
Knowing HE is greater than you.
HE goes with you. HE's always inside.

A Father

I am there as my children are born.
Feeling helplessness and awe.
I need to be there for them,
When life leaves them sore.
Saying, it's all right, everything will be OKAY.

Grown now, going their separate way.
Yet with problems, they still come to me today.
I strive for GODLY counsel, wisdom to share,
But the words that give comfort are simple words that say.
It's all right, everything will be OKAY.

My children now have children,
I love to watch them play.
When their little lives go wrong,
My children lift theirs and say,
It's all right, everything will be OKAY.

On that final day, when earthly wisdom is of use to me no more,
Then it will be my turn to hear my FATHER say,
It's all right, everything will be OKAY.
I AM *with you now for an eternal day.*

I Never Got the Chance

To and in memory of Pastor R. Bruschi, Senior

I never got the chance
To say that last goodbye
To hold you with my heart
To share your pain and cry

I never got the chance
To show the respect I feel
For me to have the honor
To pray with you and kneel

I never got the chance
To see you once last time, so now
'Til always cherish
The vision of your prime

To see your smile while preaching the Word
To see your heart in the prayers you prayed
To see the love of GOD come through
To see the light of JESUS in you

Because I never got the chance
To bring my love to an end
You've shown me something lasting
My pastor, my mentor, my friend

You've shown me that love
Should have no final goodbyes
You've shown me that love
Has nothing to do with my eyes

You've shown me that love
Lasts far beyond the earth
Those whom GOD has given me
Is simply to prove loves worth

Although you're no longer here
You are still showing me things, calming my fears
Like how to keep on loving
How to deal with pain and tears

So to one who is deserving of all my respect
In spirit I do bow
Knowing that it's not important
I never got the chance

Because of you, I know that now

His Words
Visions
Dreams
Prayers

Prayer to My Lord

My FATHER, who is in heaven,
Holy and exalted is YOUR name.

YOUR SPIRIT come into my life.
YOUR will be done in my life
As YOUR will is done throughout creation.

Thank you, FATHER, for my daily bread.
The bread of life,
My LORD and SAVIOR, JESUS CHRIST.

Thank YOU for the bread
That comes to me
From the good earth YOU created.

You forgive the wrongs I have done to others.
As I learn to forgive wrongs done to me.
YOUR forgiveness teaches me mercy and grace.

LORD, keep me from temptations of the evil one,
The temptations of the world,
The temptations of my own making.

You free me from the traps of temptation.
You free me from the penalty of sin.
Thank YOU.

Everything I have is YOURS, for everything is YOURS.
All power, all glory, all honor belong to YOU.
Now and into eternity.

Amen.

Help Me

LORD, help me to see
that which is displeasing to THEE.

For it is these very things
which holds down my hope, my joy.

Grant that the snares of enemies within and enemies without
will be made known to me.

Once known, help me to strike firmly and repeatedly,
in THY might, until all displeasure is gone,
until all enemies are defeated.

That THY help to me so manifest
that the enemy's strength over me will be broken.

Then my hope and my joy can soar to THEE,
my GOD who delivered me.

With praise and thanks as a fountain from my heart
with greater love for my REDEEMER.

Thank YOU, O LORD,
For helping me.

Emmanuel

EMM ("with") *ANU* ("us") *EL* ("GOD")
"With us is GOD"
"GOD is with us"

LORD, preserve our lives by YOUR grace.
LORD, restore us by YOUR mercy.
LORD, guide us by YOUR love.
Let this knowledge of YOU grow in our lives and our families.

LORD, YOU are the only true hope.
Help us to raise our inner eyes to see,
Clear our minds to understand,
Open our hearts to YOU.

We give all to YOU.
Knowing YOU will make all things beautiful in YOUR time.
We lean not on our own understandings.
Thereby trusting in YOU to order our lives.

We believe in YOUR sovereignty.
All YOUR ways, LORD, lead to YOUR glory.
All YOUR ways, LORD, lead to salvation of YOUR atonement.
All YOUR ways, LORD, lead to eternity in YOUR heaven.

As YOU command the winds and the water and they obey,
Command the circumstances and times of our daily lives.
LORD, YOU are EMMANUEL
GOD is with us.

The Dream

We have all had dreams that make no sense. Dreams that leave us asking, what was that about? I had been plagued by a rash of these dreams and begun to pray if GOD could stop these dreams and instead give me dreams of HIM, HIS SON, HIS SPIRIT, HIS WORD. One night, after praying this, I had the following dream in which I was not in the dream but a witness to it.

I was back in ancient times and beheld a very old man. His back was hunched over with rounded-forward shoulders, a white beard around his wrinkled leather face. I seemed to know that people would come from all over and ask to see his back. He would turn and lift his garment to reveal a back marked with stripes on his upper back from the beatings he had taken as a young man, and his lower back was marred by a large patch of blackened skin as if burnt by fire. These sores, still visible, had never healed 100 percent—such was the severity of the abuse and suffering he had endured. In fact, he should not have survived the ordeals he went through, and that is why people came to see him, to see the sores and marvel that he was still alive.

I watched as a visitor came and asked to see the old man's back. He turned and lifted his ragged garment to reveal his back. He would always do this no matter who would come and ask. He did this so that people would see what GOD had done for him in saving his life and, hopefully, come to believe in GOD. On this occasion, the visitor mocked and scorned the old man. After having done so, the visitor was instantly changed into a serpent-type creature—part human, part snake—and was to spend the rest of his life slithering along the ground. I knew that this had happened before to countless other visitors.

Then another visitor came—a beautiful young woman. She asked to see his back, and as he had done countless times before, he turned his back to her, raised his garment, and revealed his still festering sores. The young woman was visibly shaken, then drew closer and gently placed her hand on the blackened area of his lower back. Her heart was filled with compassion. She moved around and stood in front of him, looked him straight in the eyes, and said she was truly sorry.

I could somehow see in her heart that she was sincere in her sorrow. Instantly, her youth and beauty began to fade away, and she became an old woman with a hunched back, rounded-forward shoulders. Her skin became as wrinkled leather and her hair white. She continued to look him straight in the eyes and said, "I am here for you," meaning that I give myself to you to become as you.

The old man covered his back, bent down, and picked up a small bundle of firewood he had been collecting. He placed the wood in her arms and said, "Go into my house and make ready to receive me."

I remember thinking, within the dream, that he did not thank her but commanded her. She went without question, with joy and gladness in her heart, even though she had lost all her youth and beauty.

I awoke and lay there in the darkness, trying to make sense of this. After several minutes of going over and reviewing the dream, now in my awaked mind, I thanked GOD for giving me the dream, for I know that this dream came in response to the prayer I had made. I asked the LORD, "What do YOU want me to understand from this?" This was what was given.

The old man is CHRIST, not that CHRIST is old but that what was done to HIM did happen within the framework of time long past. The stripes become obvious at that point, and the area of blackened skin represents the sins that CHRIST carried, and CHRIST's new sins are always being added. The constant flow of seekers are the many people who come to CHRIST, wondering about HIM. The lifting of the garment shows that CHRIST will always reveal HIMSELF and show how HE suffered for all of us. This HE will do for all who ask HIM.

The first visitor represents those that after seeing CHRIST mocked and scorned, they do not believe but reject HIM. They become spiritual snakes, spending their lives never having raised their heads above the dust of the earth, with their minds never rising above, their spirits never developing past a physical existence. Their souls neglected and lost by their own free will.

The second visitor, the young beautiful woman, is one who will come, see, believe, and with great compassion and sincerity give themselves to CHRIST. The woman also represents all of mankind, in that both men and women come forth from woman. Her depth of sincerity and expression was to show her wish to love CHRIST and to be with HIM, in her words, "I am here for YOU." Meaning, that I am here not just to be with YOU for a brief time but to stay with YOU always. In short, her desire was to become CHRIST's intimate partner and, in so doing, had to give up who she was and become more like HIM, not to give ourselves for HIM but to become like HIM—in another sense, to mirror CHRIST. What follows is her transformation from a young beautiful woman to an old, bent-over, withered person—the reflection of the old man in the dream. This represents that which causes us to give up what and who we are and to do this with gladness and joy, to truly sacrifice what we are in order to become like CHRIST. When that happens, CHRIST gives us what HE is carrying in that we get to share in HIS work and bids us to go into HIS house and prepare to receive HIM. That is, to be ready when HE comes. CHRIST does not thank us for coming to HIM but commands or sends us in a new direction to work for HIM, to wait for HIM, and to make ready for HIM.

As I continued to lie there in the dark, with a tear in my eye, I whispered the words, "JESUS, I am here for YOU." Later, as I was putting this all down, it dawned on me that not only has HE given me the dream but he has also shown me the interpretation, so now I ask, what am I to personally understand? What more am I to get out of this beyond the interpretation?

What came back in a flash was the line spoken by the young lady, "I am here for YOU." To be *there* for your wife, your family, your friends, your pastor, your church, your job, your whatever is good but not good enough. I need to be there for CHRIST as HE was there for me. I need to show that, "I am here for YOU, LORD"—to be with YOU, to stay with YOU, to become like YOU.

CHRIST shows all of us, tells all of us, "I AM here for you."

A Dream or a Reality?

I am asleep. Suddenly, I feel awake, but I can see myself still sleeping in my bed. I can see my body lying there in my room, on my bed, under the covers.

I look above me and watch as the ceiling disappears, only to be replaced by what seems to be a universe of stars. I am drawn upward, flying through this vast expanse of stars. There is no fear but rather extreme exhilaration, total freedom.

Next, I find myself standing in a vast open expanse—the stars still overhead and a floor of black, shining glass stretching out before me. Ahead of me, there is a wall of the same black glass, reaching into the stars. I know that there is something beyond this wall, but I also know that I am not being allowed to see past it. I know that I am not allowed to see what lies beyond.

Before the wall stands thirteen thrones arranged in a wide semicircle—a great throne in the middle with six lesser thrones stretching out on either side of it.

Each throne is distinct—a mixture of wood and gold with intricate carvings. On these twelve lesser thrones sit twelve elderly men with long, flowing white beards and clothed in robes of brilliant white. The middle throne appears vacant with the exception, or more accurately a feeling, of a presence upon it. Again, there is no fear present in this place but a sense of awe, of wonder and majesty. There is only a feeling of peace and security.

The twelve men leave their thrones and approach me, forming a smaller semicircle around me. Each is holding a tall wooden staff also intricately carved, each different from the other. I am told without words being spoken, but by words appearing in my thoughts as it were, that I am to be summoned and sent.

I am instantly back in my room, physically wide-awake and fully aware of what has just happened. There is still no fear, not even bewilderment, just this feeling of awe continued, that something wonderful and completely real has just taken place. There is no doubt in my mind of the reality of what has happened.

For many nights after this one, I tried to get myself back to that place, tried to will myself there, telling myself before I went to sleep that I want to go back, wanting to fly through and past the stars and return, but I could not.

One night, after I had given up wanting this to happen again and feeling that it probably was not real after all, it did happen again. I found myself flying past the stars and back in this exact same place. Only now, before me and in front of the thrones was a great square table. It was made of the same intricately carved gold and wood as the thrones and the staffs. On this square table was a large thick book made entirely of solid gold. I was allowed to touch the cover of the book and found the gold to be soft as silk to the touch.

The twelve men again left their thrones and came to me. The book was opened before me, and when opened, it fit perfectly on the table, being of the same dimensions of the square table on which it rested. There was room for nothing else on the table. Why this was made important to me at that time? I do not know. I now know this is because within the WORD OF GOD there is room for nothing else.

The pages were turned before me as the pages would turn in any other book, and I remember thinking, *How does solid gold turn as paper?* But they did.

I was told, again by thought, not words, where to read. After I had read what they wanted me to read, my eyes would automatically look up away from the page, as if my eyes knew on their own that they were not allowed to read any further.

What I was allowed to read and understand was beyond imagination and belief. I cannot relate what I read, for after I was sent back, I could remember nothing of what I was shown in the great book. This happened on and off again for several nights. How many? I do not recall.

On another visit to this place, I asked (by thought and not spoken word) the elders, as my mind now understood them to be, "Why am I not remembering what I am being shown here?"

I was told that it is not permitted to bring this knowledge back to the earth, for if I was allowed to bring this knowledge back, then all mankind would have to believe in CHRIST, that they would have no choice but to believe, and that is not how GOD wants it. GOD wants all men to come to that decision of belief in HIM and HIS SON on their own.

Finally, on what turned out to be the final visit to this place, I was told that I was being shown this knowledge so I could personally know and believe. Then I was given the words: "That everything written about JESUS in the BIBLE is true, and this knowledge, these words, you can take back with you."

After that, I was sent back and have never returned or been summoned to that place again.

I am now passed my sixty-fifth birthday, and this happened some forty odd years ago, and yet I know that this is true and as real and still as vivid in my mind as if it just happened. In all honesty, did I believe right away? I would say, "Yes, I did believe, but it did not change my life overnight. However, a process did begin, and unwavering belief takes time. I came to accept JESUS CHRIST as my personal LORD and SAVIOR, to come to a knowledge of GOD as FATHER, and a willingness to be convicted and taught by HIS HOLY SPIRIT."

I pray this process also takes place in your life so this becomes real to you: "That everything written about JESUS in the BIBLE is true."

May 7, 2020—Dream on the National Day of Prayer

Woke up about four in the morning of May 7. Did scripture readings and some prayer. Went back to bed knowing that it was the National Day of Prayer and prayed for the nation. Of course, I fell asleep and then had the following dream.

I was watching an archeological dig. The site was of a fortified stronghold. As the digging progressed, I saw skeletons in a row on what appeared to be a ledge within the building, the type of which one would see as an old castle battlement. All the skeletons were in a half-sitting, half-lying position, showing that they died, as they stood and fought, was the feeling I received. As debris was removed and the skeletons were completely uncovered, it was revealed that there were no material remains with them—no boots, clothing, weapons, rings, watches, and personal artifacts of any kind. Everything they owned had held close, had been taken from them. The bodies were stripped bare and left as they were where they were. There was no attempt to move, bury, or honor the dead. It was shown to me that the stronghold had been simply bulldozed over on top of itself in order to be covered up and forgotten. There had been no attempt to identify the dead, no markers, no remembrances, no regrets or sorrows. All was left only to be revealed many years later.

I then found myself to be partially awake, and yet somehow still within the dream. It was at this point that I felt the following feelings or impressions.

This stronghold and the deaths were not the result of some external conflict as in one nation attacking another, but it was result of an internal cultural and spiritual conflict. This is the reason for the cover-up of the site and no memorial.

I then strongly felt the presence of a voice and was told: **"I am *not doing this. You are burying your own nation from within with your sins and surrenders of* my *ways. You are giving up the freedoms and the way of life that I had blessed you with. The things without cannot harm you, for I made your nation strong. You are destroying yourselves from within. The good I gave you is being attacked, left for dead, stripped bare, unhonored, and forgotten."***

At this point, I found myself to be now fully wake and began to pray for a revival for our awaking to the Lord, his Word and his ways—a revival not for believers only but a revival so strong that it moves the national spirit. May the Lord intercede for us or from us destroying ourselves. We can change our ways, reverse and restore what is lost, but it needs to be based on our national roots or foundations and, most importantly, on that which is higher than us.

I cannot help but think of Ezekiel and the Valley of Dry Bones. We may very well be, as a nation, on a ledge of losing ourselves by dying to a new reality, one that is stripped of all godliness. Hopefully, for those who come after us, there is a promise of some future rediscovery of what was lost, what we did, and what we are doing to ourselves. It is quite possible that we are ancient Israel in the modern era.

"Those who cannot remember the past are condemned to repeat it."

A Prayer for Our Nation and Leaders

Not to any of us, O Lord, but to Thy name give glory and honor.
Those who mock us say, where is your GOD?
The fools say, there is no GOD!
We know our GOD is real and reigns forever.
Our GOD is all wisdom, truth, power, and authority.
By Thy righteousness, establish justice and heal this nation.

Our leaders have eyes, but their actions are blind.
Lord, open their eyes to Your presence.
That they may see and do Thy good for the nation.

They have ears but are deaf to all honesty and truth.
Lord, grant them the ability to hear truth and Thy Word.
That they may hear those who cry out for righteousness.

They have mouths but speak deception and outright lies.
Lord, touch their lips with burning coals from Your Holy Fire.
That they may speak truth to all people.

They have hands that work emptiness by their empty spirit.
Lord, stretch out Your hand to guide theirs.
May their works become good, right, and spirit-filled.

They have minds but do not think of the good of the nation.
Lord, turn their thoughts toward good for the whole nation.
That they may become statesmen and not politicians.

They have hearts but do not feel.
Lord, soften and open their hearts to accept You.
That they may save themselves and reestablish Your laws.

They have power and influence but seek only self-serving ends.
Lord, open their spirits to accept the heart of a servant.
That their motives be to serve not some but all.

Lord heal, revive, restore, and refine this nation,
That we may once again turn to You.
That by Your power and through Your Spirit
We may establish the godly city on the hill You envisioned.

Messages

"Everyone who is proud in heart is an abomination to the LORD" (Proverbs 16:5).

Pride is of man's belief in only himself—secular humanism in its highest form.

"Pride believes in yourself to work and accomplish through no other power than your own. Pride does not acknowledge MY *creation and how I can work in your life. I cannot do any work through one who has pride; therefore, it is considered a deadly sin. Pride blocks* ME *from coming to you, getting through to you. Without* ME, *you die in your sin, the sin of pride."*

"Resist the devil and he will flee from you" (James 4:7).

That is the often quoted second half of that verse. First comes submission: "Submit therefore to GOD" is the first part of this verse. After you are submitted to GOD, then in HIS strength, in HIS power, you can resist the devil, and he must flee from you.

"MY words are being taken out of context; half verses are being used in order to make MY SPIRIT *fit into your philosophy. I* AM *not the* GOD *of incomplete thoughts, and* MY *meanings are not open to your personal interpretations. Instead, pray and search out meanings through* MY SPIRIT, *and by* MY SPIRIT, *I will teach you."*

Those who call themselves believers, Christians, followers of the LORD JESUS CHRIST must be always on constant guard against those who lie, deceive, and attempt to mislead.

"Beware of those who speak falsely about ME, *for their end is destruction and your end shall be suffering and pain in this life and the life to come. Do not run after* MY HOLY SPIRIT *as in,* GOD *is moving over there, let us go, or there is an outpouring of the* SPIRIT *over here, let us go. My* SPIRIT *will come to you and meet your where you are if you desire it. The only place you need to go is to* ME *in prayer, and I will come to you. For those who are working through the flesh will attempt to come to* ME *by the flesh, but those who are in the* SPIRIT *will come to* ME *through the* SPIRIT."

"You must have as much joy in the presence of the wife or husband I gave you as you would have in ME. *For if you cannot have joy in their presence, how do you expect to have joy in* MY *presence?*

I AM *going to expect more of you than they do.*

I AM *going to demand more of you than they do."*

"You can't just root out the things that you don't like in you. You need to root out the things that I don't like in you. This is the only way that your nature can become like MINE.

You can't be a believer in name only. What will it take to be a believer? To show MY *nature? Have you asked yourself this question?"*

"Blessed are those who have not seen and believed. Do you want to see ME? *Believe first. Next, manifest* MY *love. The time is not yet for you to see* ME *with your eyes, but you can see* ME *with your heart and help others to see* ME *with their hearts. This is done by your love. By* MY *love.* MY *heart in you.*

Be a person who will love ME *and then I can love through you. No matter how small your love seems to be, give it to* ME *and I will increase it, and together, we can mightily love others."*

"Stop leaving your footprint so that I can leave MINE. Pour out MY love. Pour out MY presence. Give what I have given you, for I freely gave to you so that you can freely give to others. Take it, accept it, use it, show it.

That's part of what accepting ME is all about You just don't accept ME for yourself, but you accept ME for others in your life as well. Let your actions, your words be MINE. Give ME all of you, and I will give you all of ME. Let ME exist through you. Let ME live in you so that you can let ME out.

This is what is meant by leaving MY footprint."

"This nation has turned away from ME and says we no longer follow the LORD, we no longer live by HIS laws. Therefore, we are free from HIS judgments because we do not believe in HIS power. Our nation is rich and strong, and we make our own laws and set our own morality, we can set our own standards for ourselves.

You, blind fools! Do I cease to exist because you cease to believe in ME? Do MY laws become invalid because you no longer choose to follow them? No one has ever escaped MY judgments. Forsake MY laws, MY morals, MY standards, and MY ways, and you forsake ME, for I AM in them. They are life and health and prosperity to everyone and the nation.

Yet, I have an inheritance in this land that I will claim and raise up above the fools. People will look to those who know ME and hate them on the outside but be amazed and jealous within. For the fools will see that the lives of those who come to ME are right and good. The fools will want this in their lives but be unable to accept how MY people, MY inheritance, came to have it, for they ceased to believe and, even worse, refuse to believe."

O LORD, grant that YOUR eyes see what mine see.

"This is the way it is, for nothing is hidden from ME; but the way it should be is that your human eyes see what MINE see. Think of the difference. I see the hidden thing, I see the invisible things, I see the things that need to be done in the realm of SPIRIT.

If you could see with MY eyes, then you would manifest MY presence so that MY works would be done through you and I would once again walk the earth.

Do you want to do something great for ME? Then love the LORD your GOD with all your heart and all your mind and all your soul and love your neighbor as yourself.

Manifest MY love to others. The biggest question is, the one where everyone falls short is—did you manifest MY love to others?"

Song from a Dream

It's heaven I long for

My JESUS to see

My soul belongs to JESUS

For all to see

My soul belongs to JESUS

HE has not forsaken me

My soul belongs to JESUS

HIS salvation is free

YOU are my rest for me

YOU are my destiny

For all eternity

Thoughts—Short and Long

A Thought on the Word

John 1:1

The Word brings about creation, which begs the question, why?
The Word tells us that in the beginning, there was the Word.
The Word is the beginning of creation.
The Word which is spoken is the bringing forth of existence.
So, why was the Word spoken?

All of creation—the universe, the seen and unseen, time, space, matter,
humankind, thoughts, feelings, etc., everything!
All existence is a manifestation of presence, whether physical or spiritual.
The presence of what? Even before the Word was spoken, there had to have
been something else there—someone else present. Did there not have to be
someone to speak the Word? The speaker is GOD.

"In the beginning was the Word and the Word was with GOD; and the Word was GOD" (John 1:1).

Even before GOD spoke, the Word there must be more to it.
This is to say, to wonder why, to wonder what is the reason for the Word to be
spoken in the first place.
Could that something possibly be love? If love was the reason for the Word to be
spoken, if love is the cause of the Word of creation, love must come from
someone, for love can only come from a living being. That living being, in the
beginning, before all creation, is GOD.
The speaker is GOD, the living being is GOD, even before the beginning—GOD is.
So, in the beginning, maybe the word GOD spoke was "I AM."
Maybe the Word was "GOD."
Maybe the Word was "MYSELF."
Maybe the Word was *"Let there be—"* (Genesis 1:3 and following).
Maybe the Word was *"Yes, I am coming quickly"* (Revelation 22:20).
Maybe it is every word in between those verses.

Or could it be that the love of GOD was cause enough to bring into existence all
that was, all that is, and all that there is to come. All by HIS power in one Word.
Maybe the one single spoken Word was indeed the Word of love.

"The WORD, I AM, GOD, MYSELF, LOVE."
Maybe it matters not, for in the end, all these words are in many ways the same.

Divine Word, Divine Truth

Matthew 13:3–23

When a DIVINE word, a DIVINE truth of GOD touches your mind, if it does not alter your thinking, then that revealed word of truth may pass from your thought and, as such, does not grow within you.

When a DIVINE word of GOD touches your mind, it may touch your heart for the moment, but again, if it does not affect your character and grow within you, if the word does not get planted there, then the revealed word may wither and not remain in your heart and does not change you.

When a DIVINE word touches you, it should create a change in your mind and heart—a change that remains and grows in your thoughts and emotions as it becomes a part of your life. It should affect you and influence others as the word, as a seed planted, grows you in CHRIST.

When a DIVINE word, which is DIVINE truth, touches and changes both mind and heart and you allow it to do, the SPIRITS work within you, then it can be said that HIS word has truly touched your soul, caused you to grow, and has become part of a new you.

One of greatest of an infinite number of DIVINE truths is this: That JESUS CHRIST is each person's personal SAVIOR, TEACHER, HEALER, and LORD. This becomes a never-ending string of blessings, both seen and unseen.

For not all blessings are clearly visible at once. Some blessings work quietly as they grow in your life until they can break though the surface of your life to reveal themselves to you and for others.

When this DIVINE truth, DIVINE word, touches you and plants itself as a seed in your spirit, then the blessings it brings forth grows and becomes real and true to you. Then it becomes real and true for everyone else in your life. For when you have the harvest from the seed, then those around you share in the bounty.

Thoughts on What If

What if GOD was to take you totally into HIMSELF?
What if HE was to pick up, with gentle care, boundless sympathy, forgiving love, mercy, and grace, all the broken pieces of your life?
What if HE took those broken pieces and used them again?
To put your life back together.
To remake the broken pieces into something beautiful again.
What HE puts back together is more than just the old repaired.
Using the old pieces, HE adds new things. Things different, better, stronger.

"Behold, I make all things new again" (Revelation 21:5).

This time, HE even makes it easier to find HIMSELF within you.
To become the you HE intended you to be.
HIM along with you, repaired now.
That has to be much better, right?

Your sin is repaired with HIS forgiveness.
Your failure is repaired with HIS success.
Your fallen spirit is repaired, lifted up with HIS SPIRIT.
Your despair is repaired with HIS hope.
Your life is repaired by your life yielded to HIM.

You broke, ignored, the old covenant HE had with you.
HE gives you a new covenant. Another chance. New hope.
You were broken, but HE makes you anew.
HE gives you the new you. From the inside out.
Better than the first you.

What if JESUS was to take you totally into HIMSELF?
The question is no longer, what if?
The answer is "JESUS does!"

John 1:16

"For of HIS fulness we have all received, and grace upon grace."

We just don't receive HIS grace, but we receive grace upon grace upon grace in what becomes a never-ending sentence. HIS grace is not just a onetime gift, HE gives it again and again and again in what becomes another never-ending sentence—for HE never stops giving it!

HE gives it in ways we can see.

HE gives it in ways we cannot see,

The higher spiritual ways.

The invisible ways that touch our lives.

HIS salvation is grace.

HIS HOLY SPIRIT is grace.

HIS healing is grace.

The husband, wife, father, mother, brother, sister, children that are in your life are all HIS grace.

All this and so much more.

The list goes on and on.

Each one's list is different and yet, in so many ways, the same, for all the ways HE works in our lives are examples of the fullness, the abundance, the overflowing of HIS grace upon grace.

From 3:00 a.m.

Good Moring, GOD, I love you.
"I love you too" (*Romans 6*).

GOD cannot allow any sin to enter heaven.
It would be contrary to HIS nature.
To enter heaven, you must be freed from all sin.
You cannot do this on your own.
Can a dying man give himself life?
If you could give yourself salvation,
then could you not give it to others?

Salvation cannot be given by one who needs salvation.
Salvation is not within your ability to give.
Salvation comes only by your willingness to receive.
Salvation must come from another source.
Salvation must come from someone else.
Salvation is forgiveness and freedom.

This can only be given by another living being.
This needed to be done in a way that man could understand.
Man needed something his mind could grasp.
Someone to see, someone to hear, someone to behold.
Salvation is a gift that must be given in the form of someone to give it.

A SAVIOR.
CHRIST.
GOD'S SON.

We cannot have the thoughts of GOD.
HIS thoughts are higher, HIS ways are higher.
Therefore, HE gave an example
Away—JESUS

Can we think as JESUS thought?
Walk as JESUS walked? Talk as JESUS talked? Bless others as JESUS blessed?

I think that we can—isn't that what HE taught?

How do we bless another?
A big question, an important question.
The answer to which will define the true you.
Before you answer, ponder for a while.
What the WORD calls, Selah.
Pause and think on this.

How you bless others will determine how you will be blessed.
Unavoidable spiritual law.

Back to the question—how do you bless others?
By giving something—yourself.
Physically, mentally, spiritually sharing, loving, sacrificing.
To love without motive or restraint.
To be there when needed—to help bear a burden.
To care for in sickness—to comfort when in pain.
To sorrow in their misfortune—to rejoice in their good fortune.
This is a good start.

How you bless another will depend on them and their needs.
How you bless another will depend on you and your ability to give.
Each different and unique.

A one-on-one relationship.
GOD is one—you are the other.

Consider

Have you ever stopped to consider that GOD's wrath and judgment are as just and as HOLY as HIS mercy and grace? Consider the following.

The HOLINESS of HIS mercy and grace is just as HOLY as HIS wrath and judgment. For the end result is the same. It is the ultimate "the ends justify the means" scenario.

GOD's mercy and grace can bring you to place of HIS SPIRITUAL abiding.
HIS wrath and judgment can bring you there as well.

HIS mercy and grace forgives that which is wrong in you.
HIS wrath and judgment reveals and condemns that which is wrong in you.
This should cause you to cast it out from your SPIRIT, and once cast from your life, it will bring you to that same abiding place with HIM.

First comes HIS mercy and grace. If that doesn't work, if that doesn't get your attention, next comes HIS wrath and judgment.

Forgiveness and condemnation, mercy and wrath, grace and judgment.
How awesome that these aspects, these opposites of GOD lead you to the same place.
The place of HIS abiding presence.

Consider.

Which ¼ Are You?

It has been surmised that ¼ of all humanity does not believe in the existence of punishable sin.

Another ¼ of humanity does recognize the existence of sin but will do nothing about it. It is of no lasting consequence as they live in their own world of personal, moral relativism and/or the belief that, beyond death, there is nothing.

Another ¼ of humanity also recognizes the existence of sin and works on freeing themselves from it by working on removing sin from their lives by their own efforts and their own strength of will.

Lastly, ¼ of humanity recognizes the existence of sin and have come to know that the acceptance of the atonement of CHRIST and HIS freely given salvation is the way to have release from sin, the eternal punishment from sin, and to instead have life eternal in heaven.

The first ¾s come together and laugh at the last ¼. Which ¼ are you?
Which group would you rather be included in?

The first shall be last, and the last shall be first.

Give Not Your Soul Away

We have a soul, yet we sometimes give it away. To the world, even sometimes to Satan. Repossess your soul—it is yours. Indeed, it is you, yourself.

It is the reflection of your reality, the who you are and where you will spend eternity.

Why give that all away? Knowingly or unknowingly, willingly or unwillingly.

Why allow this to happen? Yet sadly, sometimes we do, breaking the heart of GOD.

Take possession of your soul. Transfer your ownership to CHRIST.

With patience, HE waits for you,

"*I stand at the door and knock*" (Revelation 3:20).

Do you open your door and let HIM in? Letting HIM in is the start of the process. HE brings HIS power, forgiveness, wisdom, and guidance of the HOLY SPIRIT.

Ask for HIS guidance, HIS salvation, HIS mercy, HIS grace, HIS forgiveness, and you will find all this and more freely given. Follow *the way* given, seek after your own soul. You will find it!

"*For* I AM *the way, the truth and the life*" (John 14:6).

When you do this, when you find your way back, you will see yourself, as if looking in a mirror for the first time. Finally, at last, you will really see yourself but through the eyes of your soul redeemed.

Now, will that moment in time be a reunion or a confrontation? At first, that reflection of your soul may very well ask, "What have you done to me?"

But as we retake possession of our soul, that question turns into the statement, "Welcome home!"

Why remain ignorant of the way GOD created us? The world would say you are created body, mind, spirit, soul. However, when we can attain to GOD's perspective, HE created us: soul, spirit, mind, body.

There is a vast difference between those two perspectives which, left unrealized, can become the loss of contact between you and soul that will lead to an eternal difference. Our own undisciplined physical nature can lead to this loss of contact and cause us to surrender our own soul. The process of repossession, of recontact is one of physical strength, mental courage, and spiritual discipline, along with patience and determination being worked out in the flesh first, SPIRIT second.

Don't surrender your soul. Hold onto it as your most cherished possession, for in the long run, in the eternal scheme of things, it is!

The Power of His Atonement

The atonement of CHRIST gives HIM the authority to enter into my life, rearrange it, take it over, and grant me new life. When I allow HIM to do this from that point on, all the past negative experiences of my life—the thoughts, the words, the actions—are forgiven. My life is now based on the new life with the new foundation cornerstone of HIS new life that is given to me when I accept it.

By HIS miracle, the old cornerstone of my life is removed while the edifice of my life still stands, and a new cornerstone is set in place. This is something only CHRIST can do, for HE is that cornerstone. I now have a rebuilt or resurrected life by CHRIST—here, now, and forever. A new foundation on which to set a new cornerstone upon which to build new life.

By HIS grace, I have a new spirit within and a humble spirit without because, now, I am identified with CHRIST. I allow this new identity to take over every part of my nature. The old in me must yield so the new nature in me can live.

The old man that I was is gone and a new (old) man takes its place. This is to say, not in terms of my life in years but in terms of my new life in spirit.

Yes, I can still look back and see my past. The regrets, the hurts suffered, the hurts caused, the sins committed, the opportunities missed, the times wasted, except now the difference is that I am free from all of that.

This freedom is not something I do, nor even can do, but is accomplished only by the grace, mercy, forgiveness, love, sacrifice, and power of GOD IN CHRIST.

All of which JESUS personally brought down from heaven to give to me.

When I accept it, herein begins the power, lies the power of HIS atonement.

On His Works

The works that I do shall you do also; and greater works than these shall you do; because I go to the FATHER.

—John 14:2b

What could these greater works of JESUS be, these works that we shall do?

Are they HIS many miracles? Feeding thousands? Healing? Maybe it is HIS works of forgiving, teaching, preaching, and showing others the way to a new life?

All these HE did and spoke of them—"*the works that I do.*" But HE mentioned even greater works than these! What could these greater works possibly be? Giving words of hope? Laying down our life? Loving as HE loved?

We are getting close. These are great works, but why did JESUS do them? HE did them according to HIS FATHER'S will. HE did them out of DIVINE love for all of us. A love that far surpasses human love. The greatest work that JESUS did, could it possibly be love? Loving as HE loved, I say yes, for it is this love that caused all the other works to be done.

The first work is to work in the world. Works of helping and teaching. To help others to see that the way back from sin is the acceptance of HIS salvation, to teach others by opening to them that there is truth and power in the Word of GOD, to give the gift of how lives can be changed by teaching the power of prayer, to demonstrate the reality of having a personal relationship with JESUS.

The second work, the greatest work, maybe even the hardest work, is to do all of this with unconditional love. To follow the example of all that JESUS did with HIS love for us. Loving as HE loved.

It could very well be that the greatest work that we can do—the greatest work that JESUS wants us to do is to love with HIS love.

Pray without Ceasing

It may very well be that we can do nothing for humanity or the seemingly overwhelming circumstances that are surrounding us, but it is good to know that we can be something for humanity and the issues confronting society.

No one person can really be of strong character, gentle spirit, pure motive, and a good heart without the world being the better for it somewhere, someplace, sometime, if even into the unknown future. Add to this to be a person of prayer and do not belittle the unknown and unseen importance of sincere, heartfelt prayer.

Therefore, if praying is all that one feels led to do, can do, or is able to do, then do so without thoughts or feeling of inadequacy or uselessness. Do so and do not stop!

To pray is to prove to oneself that you have faith. With a faith strong enough, we can make crooked paths straight, uproot trees, and move mountains.

Be a person of prayer.

A Thought on Thoughts

Your thoughts will shape what kind of mind you are made of.

    Your mind will determine your character.

    Your character will manifest outward into your personality.

    Your personality will set in motion the world you allow around you.

    Your world around you will shape your thoughts.

Therefore, always strive to bring your thoughts to be centered on GOD in CHRIST by the HOLY SPIRIT. Do this and your existence becomes the knowing and living of the simplicity of the gospel, the humility of faith, the promise of the gift of salvation, and the eternal life before you.

Imagine what your life could be when these thoughts become set in your mind to shape your character and build your personality that creates your world!

"*Think on these things*" (Philippians 4:7–9).

A Child's Reflection for Grandparents' Day

Grandma needs new glasses; she doesn't see as good as she used to anymore,

But without looking, she always knows when I enter the room.

How does she do that?

Grandpa needs to sit a lot more now, he can't run after and chase me anymore,

But he always comes to me to hug me hello and to hug me goodbye.

Why does he do that?

So, I guess they showed me how to see without always using my eyes and why I should always warmly greet others, especially those whom I love.

How did they do that?

Grandma likes to look at her old photos, Grandpa likes to listen to his old records.

So, I learned how to look at and appreciate those things that have happened before me and to always listen with patience and quietness.

How did they do that?

They taught me without teaching me. Not like my teachers do.

But they taught me without saying a word.

How did they do that?

I guess it's because they love me. My parents say they loved me so much as a baby, and I know they love me now that I've grown.

Because I can feel their love, even when they're not around.

How do they do that?

They've watched me grow, and I have learned to see their wisdom.

A wisdom based on years of living; a wisdom based on years of loving.

Is it maybe because they have gone through so much?

How did they manage it?

They have watched me grow and, in a way, I can see now that I have watched them grow too.

Not just grown older but gentler, with an understanding of how and why things are the way they are, and oh so patient with me.

How do they do that?

Sometimes, they almost know what the world will throw my way, even before I saw it coming.

How do they know that?

Mom and Dad say it's because they pray to the Lord and for me.

I guess it's because they're grandparents, and that's just what grandparents do. They taught me how to love by loving me, always and in all ways.

Maybe that's how they did it.

They do not know it, but I often think back on the past and hear them quietly inside my spirit, and I say to myself,

"Thank God for my grandparents."

More Mary, Less Martha

"Martha, Martha, you are worried and upset about many things, but only one thing is needed. Mary has chosen what is better, and it will not be taken away from her" (Luke 10: 38–42).

We all have a little bit of Mary and a little bit of Martha in us. We, indeed, need more of Mary's spirit. Why? Because JESUS told us so!

We are told that Martha was worried about many things. I believe that the LORD saw that it was not just the meal that she was preparing for HIM and HIS disciples that occupied Martha's time and thoughts but that there were many other things in her life that took her away from what was truly important. Did JESUS perceive that Martha was a worrier, a planner, someone who needed order and organization? A person who needed to know what tomorrow will bring? Who needed to oversee her life and, maybe, even take responsibility for others in her family? In short, someone just like us, or at least someone just like me.

Mary, on the other hand, had JESUS in her focus at that moment in time.

There JESUS was, right there in front of her. Can you picture her sitting on the floor, right there in front of HIM, hugging her knees to her chest, her eyes fixed on HIS face, hanging on every word, taking it all in. So close that she could reach out and touch HIM! Feeling but not consciously realizing that HIS presence pushes everything else out of the way, the other somethings become unimportant.

Can we see this scene from scripture in our mind's eye? Feel it in our heart? Do we long for it as Mary did? Or are we like Martha? Off doing something else, concerned about many other things, thinking other thoughts while JESUS is trying to come into our lives and teach us that which we need to hear and know and make a part of our lives.

When the best choice is right before us, why do we chose the lesser choice?

Mary made a different choice from her sister, and Martha was not happy about it! Martha, to her credit, went to JESUS with her problem, went to JESUS for an answer, hopefully the solution to her problem. The issue here is that the solution to her problem was not what JESUS had in mind. What Martha got in reply from JESUS we can be sure is not what she expected, not what she wanted to hear. Are we prepared for that same thing to happen to us?

The better choice was not far away from Martha at all. It was in her own house, just in the other room, all Martha had to do was take a few steps and find a new step of faith. Had she done so, I believe that JESUS would have welcomed her and, when HE had finished HIS teaching, would have said to all present, "Now let's all help Martha get a meal ready!"

Can We Bring This to Jesus?

We need to remember one important thing, which is, we live our lives in God's presence. Whether we know it or not, believe it or not. All that we do, say, think, feel, whether good or bad, is known to God. Nothing can be hidden from him.

We are eager to bring the problems we need taken care of to him. The money problems, relationship problems, health problems, the list of our problems goes on and on. Each list different and yet in so many ways similar, for we tend to bring whatever troubling circumstances we have in our lives to him.

We are also ready to bring the things we desire to him so that they can be brought into existence. All our mores and wants, we do not hesitate to bring to him. Here they are Lord, solve and fulfill them, and now please!

Now let us look at another aspect of bringing things in our lives before the Lord, for (excuse the expression) there is always the other side of coin.

All the things we do in our daily lives are done in his presence—they are brought also in that they are always before him and known to him.

That person we are about to be rude to, those thoughts about how wrong that person is and how right we are, that loved one with whom we are about to lose our temper. Thoughts of, "Oh, we get around this by doing that, we can do it our way instead of the way it should be done, and we can get away by not doing this at all, no one is going to notice," God knows.

We need to stop and ask, can we bring any of this to Jesus? Of course not.

But we unknowingly do it anyway because we live our lives in the presence of God, and all we do is brought before him. We are always in his presence, for we live by his grace, within his creation. It is impossible to live apart from him.

Even an unbeliever lives in God's presence. They do not understand it, like it, or believe it, but that does not change the reality of his creation in which we dwell.

God does not become invalid because we choose not to believe in him.

Neither do his laws, his ways, the life he wants us to live according to his will, none of this become invalid. The laws of God, his ways, and his will are unchangeable, unmovable, and shall always prevail.

The fact that we live and have our being, our spirit and soul, within his creation is unalterable truth, regardless if we believe it or not. We may as well make the conscious effort to live in the presence of God, for we are there anyway. Can we take our life and bring it to Jesus?

Testimonies

A testimony should no longer be that I <u>was</u> saved but that I <u>am</u> saved, and <u>you</u> can be saved as well. The truth of this becomes quite simple to understand when we witness CHRIST and not ourselves. Being saved is not a past action but a state of being of a new everyday life that reaches into the future, even into eternity.

To relate our experience of coming to salvation or what we call our testimony, others might be impressed or moved, although that is certainly NOT the goal. The goal is for us to want to awaken the other person(s) to their need for CHRIST. The thoughts of the hearer should not be, *That's great for you, how nice for you*, or even, *What does this have to do with me?* but *I want what you have, to find what you have found, to see what you see, to know what you know.*

It is not the sharing of personal experiences that saves people but the gospel of CHRIST and HIM crucified. JESUS said, *"And I, if I am lifted up from the earth will draw all men to ME."* JESUS is and must be the only draw, not us.

We need to lift up and speak of CHRIST and what HE accomplished for and what is available to the hearer, not the speaker. The hearer needs to see only himself reflected in what CHRIST did, and the reflection should be of CHRIST and NOT of the speaker. Let CHRIST be that which draws and not the path we took to get to HIM.

Have you ever been taken aback by some testimonies with the constant use of *I*? "I did this, I did that, I went, I came, I prayed," and the Is go on and on.

When we use a testimony to present CHRIST to others, it must be, "HE did this for <u>you</u>, HE did that for <u>you</u>, HE came for <u>you</u>, HE prayed for <u>you</u>, HE forgave <u>you</u>, HE died for <u>you</u>, HE arose for <u>you</u>, HE gives <u>you</u> eternal life."

Salvation is one of the most personal experiences that one can have. Therefore, it needs to be *their* experience and not ours. Our testimony must be what GOD has done, can do to bring about the hearer's salvation. What GOD has done to bring us to salvation is not as important as what HE has done, can do to bring the hearer to accepting CHRIST and HIS free gift of salvation.

If we happen to be fortunate enough to be used of GOD, that is, to be in the right place at the right time with the opportunity to witness, why witness of ourselves when you can witness CHRIST with HIS words:

"The words that I speak to you are SPIRIT *and they are life"* (John 6:63).
"I AM *the bread of life"* (John 6:35).
"I AM *the way; the truth and the life. No one comes to the* FATHER *except by* ME" (John 14:6).

A Disciple

If you are to become a disciple of JESUS, you must become one, be made one supernaturally. The process is not an easy one. Read the gospels and see what the disciples had to go through, endure, and learn.

As long as it is a conscious decision or an act of will to become a disciple by one's efforts, you can be pretty sure that you are not. This is to say that discipleship is not something that you can achieve by human effort, will, desire, and certainly not by works.

JESUS says, "*You did not choose* ME, *but I chose you*" (John 15:16). JESUS changes your nature by putting HIS nature in yours, not taking your nature into HIS. Your nature is surely incompatible with HIS. Your nature is earthly, limited, and bound; HIS is heavenly, eternal, and free.

Certainly, the process does begin by you coming to HIM and placing yourself in HIM. However, it does not stay that way—it must not stay that way for the result would be stagnation. For this process to grow and to accomplish the work of discipleship, you must allow HIM to put HIS nature into yours. The Word tells us that we must die to self. Understand that is going to take great effort and time on your part. Your work on yourself is but one of the keys to discipleship.

If you accept and allow that spiritual work to begin in you, oh my! what shall the outcome be? What will you discover? What manner of man/woman will be created by HIS divine nature within our human nature?

The answer to that question is unique to each person. Again, read the gospels and find that all the disciples were not the same.

Start the process, the journey, the quest and discover for yourself the disciple you can be.

The Ripples

GOD is like a deep water which is calm and still. Under the surface of the water are things we cannot see. The deep mysteries of the things of GOD—how HE works and why.

Outside the surface of the water is where we live. All the things we see and know, and yet the still, calm surface of the water is where our lives meet HIS, our world with HIS.

Take a stone. A stone of trouble, misfortune, difficulty, pain, grief, regret, and sorrow. Any of the stones of life that may disturb our relationship with GOD.

Cast into the water, it breaks the calm stillness, and ripples move out in all directions away from the stone.

The ripples, the movement of the water, is that which disturbs our contact with GOD. The ripples are, also in turn, GOD reordering, restoring the surface to its calm stillness.

As the ripples, a circle, move out in all directions away from the stone, so is GOD reordering, restoring our life back to its calm stillness. As the circle of ripples get larger and move away from the stone, the lives of all within our life's circle get touched, reordered, restored as well. The lives of those whom our life touches.

Yet at the same time, the ripples fade as they spread out, they get less intense, disturb less of the surface of the water, include less lives. GOD does not need to reorder and restore all of HIS creation, just our circle within it.

What of the stone? What happens to it? It sinks below the surface of the water into the depths of GOD's love. The stone is hidden, covered by HIM, never to be seen again. Never to break the surface of our contact with HIM and all those within our circle, whose lives touch ours.

Let GOD work in your life, and HE can and will restore you and all those close to you to HIS calm stillness.

Doors

John 10:9

Your life is filled with doors. One door after another. Doors of the past. Doors in the present. Doors yet to come in your future. Once you enter through one door, there is within that room more doors, and on and on it goes throughout your life.

Some doors are meant for you, and they open with ease, and yet, there are doors which are not for you. Herein lies the paradox—the doors that are not for you will still open, for GOD locks no doors. This is HIS free will, given to you, the ability to choose.

Some doors lead to happiness, the good things in life, and of course, some doors lead to despair, and you regret having opened them and entered in.

GOD knows all your doors and what lies beyond them, and HE will allow you to knock on any door at any time in your life and open it. Again, this is HIS free will, a gift to you, a gift of the freedom of choice, and it is never too late to choose anew.

The doors that lead to the good things in life, the doors that open into happiness and fulfillment, for these doors we are grateful and thankful.

But what of those other doors? The ones you never should have opened.

The ones that leave you lost and in bondage. You wonder how and why you came to this place, the doors that leave you with, "How do I get out of here?"

You try to turn around but feel as if the door has locked behind you.

Again, herein lies the same paradox—GOD locks no doors. There is always a way out, always another door. GOD will never leave you trapped someplace you do not want to be. You may not be able to go back through the same door, and why would you want to, since that door was the wrong door. But there is always another door, another room, another choice, another way.

JESUS told us that HE is the door. "I AM *the door; if anyone enters through me, he shall be saved, and shall go in and out, and find pasture*" (John 10:9).

Find the door marked JESUS. All who come to HIM will have life abundant

Are you someplace where you do not want to be? Don't remain there! There was a door that got you there, and there is a door that can get you out.

JESUS told you, "*Ask, and it shall be given to you; seek, and you shall find; knock, and it shall be opened to you. For everyone who asks receives and he who seeks finds, and to him who knocks it shall be opened*" (Matthew 7:7–8).

The asking is the knowing that JESUS is there for you; the seeking is the faith that by JESUS, you can be released and healed; the knocking is the wanting to be free and restored by the power of the risen CHRIST in your life.

It was early morning or very late at night, depending on your perspective.

I asked the LORD again, as I have done before, to please come into my life.

What came to my mind was, **"*You have to put* me *there.*"** I could not get past this as it took over my thoughts. The LORD will not force HIS way into my life, into every thought and every deed. I must put HIM there. HE will not make every part of my life holy to HIM. I must make every part of my life holy to HIM.

I cannot just want it, wanting is not enough. I need to make the presence of GOD real in my life. GOD can bring HIS presence into every part of my life when I willingly allow this to become real to me. Waiting for this to happen is not how this works. The initial action is up to me.

First, the LORD does not come where HE is not wanted. Second, because HE is the HOLY GOD, HE will not dwell with unholiness. This is not to say that HE cannot but that HE will not.

The presence of the LORD in my life is first and foremost up to me. As I open my spirit to HIS, GOD will honor that, and then HE can begin HIS work in me.

HE will knock on closed doors; those arears in my life that I have closed off to HIM. HE will knock and let me know that HE is there, waiting. HE will not open for me, for I need to open them so that HIS presence can enter in. The LORD will be standing right there in the now open door, and I can hear HIM saying:

"What took you so long, I have been waiting for you to open to me, *to want* me. *My presence is so much more than what you find in* me *in times of study, prayer, worship, and thanksgiving. My presence goes beyond* my *word, is deeper than prayer. My presence is more than singing, praising, and thanking* me *with thoughts of* me *in your mind and heart. All of this is wonderful, and I love you for it. However, I want more. As strange as it may seem, you must get past trying to only give to* me. *My presence involves allowing* me *to give to you. To be open to my presence in your life is to trust* me *so much that you hold back no part of your life to* me. *My presence is your opening all the doors of your life to* me. *Allowing* me *to look into every dark, hidden corner of your life.*

"I would love for my *thoughts to become your thoughts for* my *life to dwell within yours.*

"You want me *in your life? That is the beginning of the ability for you to see just how much I want you too. I start by giving you that desire, that need to ask. Now it is up to you. Know this also, that when you get to this point, you are starting to feel a profound spiritual truth, which I will not do to you but, more to the point, I will do it with you.*

"You must be the one to start the process. It begins with your sincere desire for me *and your honest asking of* me. *The process of more than letting* me *into your life is you wanting to put* me *into your life."*

Sets of Words

As it relates to our relationship, that is to say how we react to or interact with GOD and CHRIST, the words TEACHER, MASTER, and LORD seem to hold little place of use in our modern world. We seem to like the words SAVIOR, SANCTIFIER, and HEALER much better.

TEACHER, MASTER, and LORD require in us a response and a responsibility outward or toward. An allegiance owed with responsibilities and obligations attached. Implied is someone we need to recognize, accept, listen to, be accountable toward, and give to.

Whereas the words SAVIOR, SANCTIFIER, and HEALER make us the receiver.

We need do nothing but get from. This is so much easier to do. It fits much better into our busy, complicated lives.

The first set of words are active and outward—we must give to. That is to say we must give acknowledgment of authority, of supremacy. The second set are more passive and inward—we get from. We get something from without, which is perceived to come to us without cost.

Both sets of words are important but the second set flows from the first. The latter depends on the former. To borrow the expression "You can't have one without the other."

We can see further evidence of this by another set of words. Grace and obey. We much rather receive grace. This is much easier to do than obey—obey all that a SOVEREIGN and HOLY GOD requires of us, which we discover by and through HIS Word.

Receiving HIS grace toward us, freely given, is an easier path than us having to obey HIM and all that obedience requires.

We can see even more evidence by one last word—love. When we truly love, we expect not only to receive from but give to as well. When we truly love, we will want to pour ourselves into that love relationship. We will want to serve it in some way, show our affections, demonstrate allegiance, be obedient to all that a love relationship requires of us. In many ways, we seek to actively work within ourselves to first obtain a love relationship and then sustain it.

Therefore, the words TEACHER, MASTER, LORD, and, yes, even love will depend upon our ability to obey.

Only then is our TEACHER, MASTER, and LORD freely able to bless us with HIS saving atonement, sanctification, and healing. All of which is part of HIS freely given grace when we accept and obey.

John 2:6–11

There is the law of old which is large and empty.

Verse 6—*in that place there were six stone water jars that the Jews used in their washing ceremony.*

The stone jars represent the Mosaic law of the Old Covenant and the layers of laws that had been added on by men over the centuries. The washing ceremony is part of that law, by which the Jews of that time believed they could be made spiritually clean. The law is what they lived by; it provided the order, meaning, and purpose for their lives.

Each jar held about twenty or thirty gallons.

These were obviously large jars, and there were six of them, showing that the law had become large, cumbersome, and heavy. No one could possibly carry these jars holding twenty to thirty gallons each, symbolically making it impossible to carry or fulfill the law.

The living word is given by Jesus.

Verse 7—**Jesus** *said to the servants, "Fill the jars with water." So they filled the jars to the top.*

The jars or law stand large and possibly empty. The water is the living word of God, so what the law lacked was the living word.

At this point, the servants knew not who the man Jesus was, but they obeyed. So the servants filled the jars. This must have been no easy task and had to have taken some time to draw and carry that much water to fill the jars to the top. Not half way up but to the top, showing that the ancient law was lacking and that it is Jesus who came to fulfill the law, to make it complete, to put the spirit back into an empty set of laws and rituals.

Now, take the GOSPEL into all the world.

Verse 8—**then** he *said to them, "Now take some out and give it to the Master of the Feast."*

These servants do everything the LORD tells them to do, without questions or knowing the purpose. These servants showed us exactly what a servant should be. We have the advantage of knowing the LORD, and yet we still do not always follow HIS commands.

The master here represents those who consider themselves to be the master of their feast or the ruler of their fate, the ruler of their lives. The master here is us without CHRIST. That part of us which is worldly-minded, and the feast is life.

So They Took the Water to the Master

The servants took the water to the master or the Word to the worldly. The living word is spread. This foretells of the spreading of the GOSPEL by the faithful. By hearing the GOSPEL and accepting JESUS, one can enter into new life.

Verse 9—*when he tasted it, the water had become wine. He did not know where the wine came from, but the servants who had drawn the water knew.*

When those who are of the world taste or test the living water and accept the Word as good and true, it becomes a wine of new life within them.

The master of the feast tasted the wine or tested the Word, knew it was good, but did not know from where it came. He still did not know JESUS, but the servants or the faithful knew. JESUS will always make HIMSELF known to HIS faithful servants. The servants can draw the water or carry the Word only—it is JESUS who turns the water into wine, the Word into new life.

The master of the wedding called the bridegroom and said to him—

This first miracle takes place at a marriage, where two are joined together.

Here, JESUS becomes our BRIDEGROOM. There are those who have a problem with this because in the flesh or the world, JESUS is a guest at this wedding, not the bridegroom. What we need to see is at this point, HE becomes the BRIDEGROOM in SPIRIT. By CHRIST, the flesh is being joined to SPIRIT, man is being married or reconciled back to GOD. HIS grace is marrying us to HIMSELF. We must accept this on faith and know it to be true, for this is why HE came, that we should not look at the things of the world but only believe in HIM and HE who sent HIM.

Now the master calls the bridegroom; he does not call the servants. This tells us that once we have tested and accepted the Word as true, it is then that we can call upon HIM and go to JESUS directly.

JESUS reveals HIS glory.

Verse 10—*people always serve the best wine first. Later, after the guests have been drinking awhile, they serve the cheaper wine.*

Others give their best first and then the inferior is brought forward. When we look at many other religious leaders or founders in history, their lives and deaths did not prove their deity. They did, indeed, alter their corner of the world, but it did not affect the entire history and spirituality of mankind. Their glory fades, and something else takes its place. That something we call religion. To truly know JESUS is not a religion but a personal, intimate relationship. Only CHRIST comes back and, with new life, can change your water into wine.

The best that man has received so far, the law, was already brought forward and found lacking when compared to the new wine, the gospel of JESUS.

But you have saved the best wine till now.

It is very interesting that the bridegroom does not answer these challenges; no excuses, no explanations are given. Where else does the bridegroom not answer? At the end, at HIS trials. This is a foreshadowing of that time when JESUS easily could have answered, easily could have explained, easily could have revealed HIS power and glory, but HE did not.

JESUS became man, then HE becomes the bridegroom, and then HE becomes the LAMB. For JESUS to become the sacrificial lamb, HE has to join us to HIMSELF. Only then could the wine be poured out to all and HE could atone for our sins by our identification with HIM and HIS identification with us.

We need to look to the last miracle. When HIS side was pierced with a spear, what came out? Water and blood. CHRIST took all things upon HIMSELF, both the lower and the higher, life and death, water and blood, and as per the WORD, "The life is in the blood." HE reconciles all things within HIMSELF and by HIS shedding of HIS blood.

The entire gospel is pictured here in what is quite possibly a true-to-life parable. Meaning that this is more than a true story about HIS first public miracle retold but a prophetic story about what will come to pass and its meaning. HIS best comes later; the wine of new life is brought out or revealed at the end, not up front in the beginning of HIS ministry. JESUS started out to appear to us as a man and, in the end, CHRIST revealed HIMSELF as the LIVING GOD whom death cannot hold. The best is yet to come, the fullness of HIS glory is yet to be revealed.

You have seen, so only believe.

Verse 11—*so in Cana of Galilee,* **Jesus** *did* **his** *first miracle. There,* **he** *showed* **his** *glory, and* **his** *followers believed in* **him.**

What a confirmation! HE showed HIS glory. The first miracle points to the last—HE is the water; of the Word become the wine of new life. All that CHRIST is, is foretold in this one miracle of water into wine, and we who call ourselves HIS followers need only to believe in HIM.

I will conclude by going back to very beginning of John chapter 2, verse 1…

And on the third day—

He who has ears to hear let him hear.

To Believers Now and to Come

What would you say if I told you that you can have a simple proof that GOD loves you, has not forgotten about you, and has a strong desire for you to have a relationship with HIM? A relationship that gives proof of HIS love.

The proof is that you are reading this and feeling that pull toward wanting more, meeting other believers, reading a Bible, attending a church. You willingly think on things of the SPIRIT or worship HIM or to hear and learn of HIS word. Despite all the other things that the world has to offer you, all those other things to which you can give your precious and limited time, you are pondering, wondering, questioning, seeking. Why?

Because HE reached out to that part of you, the inner you wherein HIS SPIRIT awaits you, longs for you, and calls to you. You in turn heard the call, felt the touch, sensed HIS longing for you, thought upon it all, and responded to HIS love.

You, of course, entered life as a baby, as a child of GOD. Yet you do not go through those younger years of your life, the years of babyhood, becoming a toddler, then a young child, and even a young adult, knowing this truth about yourself. The truth that you are HIS beloved child and HE wants you to know HIM.

But all along, GOD has been preparing your return to the knowledge of HIM and HIS love for you. It is HIS desire that you be reclaimed by HIM, to return to HIM, to be born again by HIS SPIRIT. To be born again but, this time, with your knowing of the power of HIS love for you, HIS child. The beauty in all this is that HE gives you the ability to know that HE loves you. Do not overlook the evidence of this powerful proof that lies within your ability to know of HIS love.

Because of HIS love for you, HE called out to you. He loved you so much that HE maybe even had to call out several times, maybe over several years. HE wanted you to know that HE has fresh, clean water for you to taste of, as opposed to dirty, earthly cisterns. What did HE ask of you other than to know of and accept HIS love? All along, HE wanted you to hear HIS call of love to you and then see HIM with the eyes of your spirit.

If you are now able "to taste and see that the LORD is good" and that this is but a small part of HIS daily bread for you, is this not proof of HIS love?

The strength and power and ability of your belief in HIM is the proof of the love HE has for you. The proof is that you are aware of HIS love now.

Face-to-Face

Easter is a time of year for you to come face-to-face with Jesus.

The Jesus of the cross—scourged, crucified, died, buried, and arose. At this time, more so than any other, for at Christmas time, you may come face-to-face with the infant in the manger and feel the wonder and see the beauty of the newborn infant, the majesty and mystery of Christ born. But perhaps you are not yet ready or maybe even not yet willing to come face-to-face with the Jesus of Easter, the Messiah of your personal salvation. You tell yourself that I can face him sometime later on, and I will deal with him then, later when I am more ready.

In fact, there will, indeed, come that sometime later, the time of reconciliation in your life. No one knows when it will come, and hopefully, it will come while you are still here on earth. The Word of God speaks of a time when you shall confront the judgment of your sins. Your choice becomes, do you choose to confront your sins now or after you pass through the door to heaven? That door has a sign above—it that reads "Judgment," and past that door are the doors marked "Eternity in Heaven" or "Eternity of Separation." When you get to that point, the choice is already made for you. One door will open, the other will not.

Before that time comes, you must accept the mercy, grace, and forgiveness of the atonement of Christ in order to be free of your sins. If you can't or won't accept his salvation, your sins are all you will see, all you will have. Accepting the atonement of your sins by Christ gives you the ability to leave and live. To leave your sins behind and live in his Father's house.

Look up at the cross, and there, come face-to-face with Jesus. The Jesus who is beyond your sins. The Jesus that went to and came down from the cross. The Jesus that went through death and brought everlasting life back with him, to give to you. Jesus is the one looking beyond your sins, forgiven and forgotten, with Jesus seeing you and only you, looking at your face, a face cleansed and free.

Now what do you do? Do you look away, casting your gaze someplace else? Looking for a different path to that new home, another way to eternal freedom? Or are you ready to stand before Jesus, face-to-face? Jesus came face-to-face with your sins on his cross so that you could come face-to-face with him. Do you have the courage to "*look full in his wonderful face*"? If you do, then "*the sins of earth will grow strangely dim in the light of his Glory and Grace.*"

Jesus wants that face-to-face relationship with you. He wants you to look deeply into his eyes while his eyes reach in to save your soul. After you have met him face-to-face, then he comes alongside your life, putting his arm around you and saying, "Now together we can go to my Father and your Father, my God and your God." Are you ready for that face-to-face moment?

THANKSGIVING...OR...A CHAIN OF EVENTS...OR...FOR PASTORS

It is that time of the year we refer to as Thanksgiving. We reflect on this and what it means to be thankful and what it is that we are or should be thankful for; as I listen to the thankful testimonies of others, the following thoughts occur.

We thank GOD for HIS blessings in our lives. From things HE has provided for us, for situations HE has brought us through, to circumstances HE has worked out, to relationships HE has restored. The list can go on and on with each person's list being different but in so many ways the same. For you see, simply put, GOD worked in our lives, doing what HE determined and which needed to be accomplished for us in order to see HIM and recognize HIS hand at work.

We thank JESUS CHRIST for HIS salvation of our lives, for the gospel, for healings, and we basically end up repeating the same list as just mentioned. For CHRIST is the person of GOD become real to us and working in our lives.

I feel though that we rarely thank the HOLY SPIRIT. The SPIRIT OF GOD which begins the work in us which starts a chain of events. A chain of events which produces the outcomes for which we end up being thankful and giving us our testimonies. The HOLY SPIRIT leads us to CHRIST and then CHRIST HIMSELF takes us and leads us to salvation and brings us to the knowledge of our FATHER GOD.

A GOD who then embraces us. We come to know that GOD is not an impersonal far-off concept but a GOD who is real and interested in working in our lives.

These works become obvious to us, first personally and then proven to others by the words of our own testimonies.

Having said all this, allow me to circle back and add another person to this chain of events, meaning, let me suggest where this all starts. "Faith comes by hearing and hearing the word of GOD" (Romans 10:17). Through someone, you first heard the Word before you are able to have your testimony.

This whole chain of events begins with the man who stands before us each Sunday and makes the Word of GOD understandable and real to us. It may be the entire message, part of the message, a few sentences, or maybe even just a phrase; but something preached causes us to say, "Huh! Yes. I see that now. That makes sense to me now. I understand that now. I never saw that before." When this happens, the HOLY SPIRIT says, "*Ahah, I got ya!*"

It is at this point the work of the SPIRIT takes over, and that whole chain of events as stated begins. Whether it is the beginning of that moment of salvation or a renewal of the appreciation of salvation or a clearer and deeper appreciation of how to bring the FATHER, CHRIST, and SPIRIT to be more real in our lives.

It all began with "*hearing the word of* GOD," and so we ask, what can we be thankful for. We thank the faithfulness of him who gives the Word, that which has the ability to awaken the SPIRIT within us—so we say...thank you to all the pastors and teachers and for being the first link in that chain of events.

Consider the Miracle of the Birth of Jesus

The God who created the universe now a helpless baby inside the universe He created.

The Almighty God becomes the weakest of humans. The hands that stretched out the heavens can now only grasp the finger of His mother. The eyes that see all things, visible and invisible, can now barely focus. The mouth that spoke the universe into existence can now only offer up the cry of a helpless baby.

Yes. He who upholds all things by the word of His power can only make incoherent babbles while held in His mother's arms. He who is sufficient within Himself, needing nothing to continue His existence, must now nurse at His mother's breast in order to survive. He who is all-powerful now needs his diaper changed.

The eternal and immortal God becomes a temporal and limited human. How amazing is this? It is the miracle of God's love become flesh. The love of God came to us first as a baby before He revealed Himself as the Messiah of salvation by submission to a cross. Submission that led to supremacy. Helplessness that led to omnipotence. The omnipresent embodied in a single human life. The omniscient now needing to learn how to talk and walk,

The God of all creation comes down to one culture, one people, one house, one young, newly married couple. The unknowable majesty of God sheathed Himself in the soft envelope of a fragile baby. A Jewish baby, a Jewish boy, a Jewish rabbi, the Messiah, the salvation of all mankind. Emmanuel, God with us, but first a baby.

He who told Moses, "Thou shall not look upon my face, for there shall be no man see Me and live," now becomes a baby for all to come and see. All of this, all leading to the cross.

From a wooden manger to a wooden cross. We always consider and keep before us the knowledge of the gift of salvation from the cross, the atonement, the willing self-sacrifice, the submission to the will of the Father.

We come to church each week and hear this preached. The pastor ends each teaching with an altar call to accept the gift of salvation, and it is right and just that this be so.

We wear crosses around our necks, have them on our Bible covers, and place them atop our churches, and yet no one wears a little manger around their neck.

For the faithful, the cross of Christ is always before us. It stands as a symbol of our faith for the salvation given to us by a loving God becoming a baby. But what of that baby in the manger?

We only ponder Him and see Him in the form of a baby but once a year, whereas we keep the cross before us all the year. As Dickens wrote in his immortal classic *The Christmas Carol*, where the ghost of Christmas present says to Scrooge, "Mortal, the Christ child is not born in our hearts only one day a year but all the days of the year"—a great thought to keep before us.

Therefore, let us strive to keep alive in our hearts the worship we give to that special, unique baby boy born over two thousand years ago. May we make a fresh commitment to remember that baby throughout the year so that when Christmas time rolls around again, we can say:

I know of the greatest Christmas gift ever given.

Yes, I know this baby well.

It Is an Attitude, Not an Itinerary

God's will is sometimes made clear, plain, and sudden. However, I have found this to be very rare indeed, at least this has not always been my experience.

God's will is something that unfolds as I take steps of faith and very small and oftentimes what have been hesitant steps at that. I wonder how many steps I have missed due to my incorrect attitude at that time. Instead of questioning, I need to give thanks and pray. This is part of the development of my faith.

God leads me by taking me one step at a time. I know that this is for my benefit for HE knows that one small step at a time is all I can handle. God can accomplish HIS will all at once, bringing everything to its proper and correct fulfillment in a moment of time. HE knows the end from the beginning. Even if I am granted a greater, long-term vision, I can still only move forward one small step at a time.

The process is to read the Word of God, pray for direction, give thanks, take a small step. "Fools rush in where angels fear to tread" may be an old maxim, but contained therein is a great deal of spiritual truth. Angels know not to try and get ahead of where, why, and how God is working, and even if I mistakenly do just that and get offtrack of where God wants me to be at that time, in the long run, it matters not, for HE simply alters those next steps until I am on the way towards HIS will, in HIS time, once again. God's plan doesn't change, but my steps do.

Although I would love to know and see the entire path before me, it must be enough to simply believe that I am on it and am willing to accept its conditions.

God wants to reveal HIS will for me and HIS leading me may be by not telling me anything about HIS plan but by taking me there without me realizing it, and that is dependent on my attitude.

I need to stop looking for HIS plan to be revealed in full and develop the attitude of accepting that I won't know it all, can't know it all, for that is not how God works. The why, where, and how is not up to me to know or decide. All I can truly do is just take a small step, pause, wait, and see what HIS next step for me is.

God's will is not an itinerary; it's an attitude. And so, I won't look for the master plan, won't wait for the big revelation, it may never come, and in the waiting, I have missed and wasted precious time. I must develop and accept the attitude of being willing to take a small step and wait for the next small step.

Wine or Whine

Matthew 9:17. Mark 5:37–38. Luke 9:17.

Poured out wine or pouring out whine?

You cannot be made into wine if you cannot take being crushed.

You cannot choose how to be made wine (i.e., spiritually useful). The process is not yours but the SPIRIT of GOD. If the process causes whine, then the finished product will be bitter and unusable.

Are you ripe for the picking or HIS choosing? Will you allow yourself to be picked off the vine of what are currently the circumstance of your life or would you rather stay attached to the earthly vine along with everyone else? If you choose the picking, then be aware that next comes the pressing. Most would love to be picked or chosen but not wanting the next step in the process—the pressing. The pressing is where you will bring forth wine or whine.

To be made into HIS useful wine, all the parts of your everyday life must submit to HIS pressing. Be willing and ready to be thrown into the vat with the other grapes, those also chosen, and then being providentially stomped upon by HIS process, HIS presence, HIS will.

After this has been done, now comes the act of being placed in new wineskins.

It is time to be stored for a while, to ferment and become the new wine, the new teaching, the new purpose for your life. The juice from pressed grapes does not become wine overnight. The new wine needs the new wineskin, the new covering, the new you. A time of stretching out the new you, increasing in the things of the SPIRIT, this process must happen first.

You cannot put yourself back into what you once knew and believed. The skin of the grape, your old covering, your old self is now discarded. GOD has squeezed out of you that which HE wanted, discarded the rest, and placed the fruit of the SPIRIT in a new vessel for a new beginning.

Eventually will come the pouring out. This is GOD's timing, not yours. This will happen when and where GOD wants to share HIS new wine. HE chooses which life will drink of HIS new wine, the wine which is your life made new. HIS reason, purpose, and timing for the pouring out is not yours to decide. You are the vessel of the new wine only, but GOD is the wine master, the sommelier. Again, HE decides which wine is to be used, where it is to be used, when it is to be used, and how much of it is to be used. The reason and purpose of the use, the pouring out, is greater than yourself. If you are fortunate enough to be poured out, this is where you will find the purpose and reason for being made into wine.

When you can see and allow this, this is the new wine.

If you cannot, what comes forth from the process is the whine!

Your Body Is the Temple of the Spirit

"Not only must our 'inner sanctuary' be kept right with God, but also the 'outer courts' must be brought into perfect harmony with the purity God gives us through his grace," (Oswald Chambers, *My Utmost for His Highest*).

The body we are given is indeed the temple of the Spirit residing within. Consider what we know of the Temple in ancient Jerusalem, its physical composition composed of walls, gates, outer courts, inner sanctuary, the holy of holies, and how these all relate to each of us. A picture of who and what we are.

The surrounding (retaining) wall represents our physical body. That which is seen by all and contains all that within us which allows, gives, and sustains life.

The gates are our many senses. The sight of our eyes, to hear with our ears, our mouth to speak and take in nourishment, our nose to breathe air for life.

Hands that feel, both to reach out or to bring close, to give to take.

The outer courts are the connections, the meeting places if you will, between the physical, the mental, the emotional, and the spiritual. Here the realm of our physical bodies, our mental existence, our spiritual longings, and our greater world take on and become our thoughts, feelings, attitudes, emotions, etc.; we could go on with all those intangibles that make up our psyche, that make us who we are. The outer court is the place where we begin to give of ourselves, where we can offer up to God the things that are God's, the things he requires of us as seeking individuals and those things which we feel led to surrender, led to sacrifice.

As we approach the inner sanctuary, we come to the higher cognitive aspects of ourselves. Those things which we give ourselves to, the love we share, the beliefs we hold, the goals we set and strive toward. All those secret personal things that give our individual lives meaning, that inner knowing that tells us that life is higher than and beyond the wall of the body, past the gates of senses and through the outer courts of the world. This in this place of the inner sanctuary, this is where we come in order to stand before the entrance to the holy of holies.

Here is where we enter the holy of holies. That place where we find God resides. The place where we find God within and realize that he was there all along, waiting for us come.

Now let us further consider that which took place in the Temple, its purpose if you will. It is the place of worship, the first stop on our spiritual journey, the place of prayer; "*My Temple should be a house of prayer.*" Pray always.

Finally, to enter the holy of holies, which was done by only one priest at a time and only after atonement has been made for sin. Now forgiven, sanctified, and cleansed, the servant, which is us, enters, and we enter alone. No one can bring us in, no one can go with us. We come on our own, alone, only to find the one that created the Temple, us, to begin with.

On Moving On

As we move forward in life, no matter how forward our vision and movement toward our goals, we shall always find ourselves in the present moment. For where our vision will lead, no matter how sure we are on the path we will take, it is still in reality an uncertainty.

The world will tell us to have a five-year plan, but that can change in a moment of time.

A thought to keep in mind is this—in one aspect, the future never really arrives, for when it does, we find ourselves aware of only the present moment, the remainder of our future is still out there, awaiting its arrival into the next present moment. Only the present moment is controllable and even this to only a certain degree.

Other thoughts to keep in mind are those of the importance of our past experiences. For it is only our past that is fully knowable. The experiences of the future cannot be drawn upon, we can only learn from the experiences of our past.

Our past has brought us to who we are today, right here, right now. We must never forget our past for it has already determined not only who we are but will also affect who we are to become and to where it will lead our lives.

All the past events of our lives, both the good and bad, have something to teach. Never forgetting who we are and from where we came is the key to moving on.

Future time is but a plan awaiting.
Present time is what currently is.
Past time is bringing us to both.
Time to move on.

Those who cannot remember the past are condemned to repeat it.

—George Santayana

Only from HIM

It is only from HIM that you can find a real faith and, with it, the true reason, the true purpose, the true satisfaction, the true goal, the true path for your life.

His faith is first, and yours flows only from HIM. Let all that you do begin with HIM, flow from HIM, work out through HIM, and end in HIM. Faith.

It is good but also not enough to strive to live for HIM; we have to live from HIM. The difference? To live life as HE gives it—by HIS ways, HIS words, HIS morals. That, in and of itself, can be a great undertaking, requiring great endurance, patience, and, most of all, faith! Part of faith is to find within yourself the ability to act from HIS action, to feel from HIS heart, to see with HIS eyes, to be from HIS being, to become who you are from whom HE is. This is not an easy task, an easy life, but it is possible. How? Because HE put that faith inside you.

Find it and learn the secret of living from HIS love, HIS faith. What is this secret? To live in a manner worthy of the love CHRIST has for you. HE wants you to cast away from your outer life the life that others see, anything that has no place in your life with HIM. Then move on and remove from your inner life anything that has no place being in your mind, your heart, your spirit. Live each moment as HE would have you live it, and that requires you to be open to HIS leading, HIS words. Accepting what HE has for you by faith.

Again, not easy but possible. No one ever said, including JESUS, that this would be an easy way to follow, an easy way to live. Real faith is not easy, so do not expect an easy faith and don't give up when faith doesn't happen right away. The walk on the path of faith will be hard going, not impossible.

You can live on earth with the presence, the love, and power of heaven in your heart and, therefore, in your everyday life. Walk in the newness of life that comes from HIS salvation. Walk in the newness of life that comes from keeping HIS words on your mind and in your heart.

Step out of your old ways and habits, step off the old paths walked. Do what you have never done before but should have done, step on the pathway of a reborn life, which is the renewal of your life by HIS HOLY SPIRIT made real in you.

You can have all of this, you can find your faith, you can accept and have a life made new, but only from HIM.

The Invitation

Most of us have received an invitation to a wedding or are at least familiar with one. Let us look at what is sent to you, received by you.

You get the invitation to the ceremony itself; the two who are being joined together, along with the time and the place of the joining. Then you will also get the invitation to the celebration that is held after the vows are made and the two have become one. Usually, there will also be the directions to the place of the celebration and, finally, the response card with a self-addressed stamped envelope with which to reply.

Even if you have never received an invitation to an earthly wedding, GOD has invited you to join with HIS SON and with HIM in a spiritual wedding. Unlike an earthly invitation, this one is a long-standing invitation that will never be taken away—it is good for your entire life, and you can accept it now, why hesitate with your response?

GOD has invited you to life eternal with HIM, free from sin and its punishment. His invitation is always there, awaiting your acceptance. HE will never take it back from you, and HE sends you a new one every day if you ignore the first one.

When you get there, you will find that the bridegroom is JESUS CHRIST and the bride is you. The FATHER wants the two of you to be joined together. The joining is in your heart—the place is here, and the time is now. It matters not if you are man or woman, for HE wants all of us to be joined with HIM through HIS SON so that we may come to know them both. GOD wants all of us to accept HIS invitation to receive HIS gift of salvation. GOD even provides the gift.

You also get the invitation to the celebration that will come after the joining. This celebration is a life renewed now with salvation from sin and a life eternal in heaven.

Just as an earthly wedding, you need to be present for the joining first, where the two become one, before you go to the celebration. The spiritual joining is necessary to attend the spiritual celebration. You cannot attain the one without first attending the other. You cannot go to the reception without taking part in the wedding. You cannot have life eternal without accepting HIS invitation of salvation.

GOD also gives us the directions on how to get to the wedding and reception. You will find the directions when you accept HIS invitation. The directions are in HIS Word, HIS gospel given by JESUS and delivered to you by HIS HOLY SPIRIT.

This brings us to the response card. It does not cost you anything to send it back, and you gain the threefold joy of being part of the new union and the celebration and the gift that comes along with your acceptance.

The response card is you and what you do with HIS invitation. Do you want to go to the joining ceremony and the reception awaiting you? Do you want to receive your gift? Send your response with a "YES, I accept YOUR invitation and YOUR salvation."

In your heart, accept what GOD has done for you by HIS GRACE through HIS SON. The three of them: GOD the FATHER, the bridegroom, JESUS CHRIST, and the HOLY SPIRIT are waiting to hear from you. Let the celebration begin!

On Adult Baptism

Acts 2:1–21

Baptism as an adult uses water as a symbol; JESUS told HIS disciples that they would be baptized with the HOLY SPIRIT. This came during the celebration of Pentecost. Your baptism or your own personal Pentecost, if you please, is to show you have accepted the salvation of CHRIST. Do not ignore it or put it off.

Adult baptism is the symbol of something more than your acceptance of the great and free gift of salvation and an eternity in heaven. It is also to make you, to transform you, to bring you into a new life, into the life of a believer, into a servant for GOD in CHRIST. To the apostles that day, it was the receiving of power in the SPIRIT sent by CHRIST.

You become a message in the flesh with the ability to witness for CHRIST with your new you, your new life. To give you a new tongue or new manner of speech with which to speak of the forgiveness your received, the salvation you received, HIS mercy and grace given to you, the promise of heaven secured.

To grant you the blessing of having that ability, an unseen SPIRITUAL fire may rest upon you to cause others to comprehend in their spirit and come to believe as you now believe.

At Pentecost, the baptism of the HOLY SPIRIT came as a mighty wind to those who already believed, and flames of SPIRITUAL fire rested upon them, not for their own good, for they already believed, but *"for those who do not believe, for those who need their belief encouraged,"* to maybe catch a glimpse of GOD. For the HOLY SPIRIT does not only come to you alone, for your own good, but the good of others with whom you will meet as you journey through life. For your glimpse may grow into a greater vision for others to come to see, come to believe in and accept their own salvation.

When you accept HIS salvation and submit to the baptism of the HOLY SPIRIT, you will go and become a blessing to others.

"Go therefore and make disciples of all nations, baptizing them in the name of the FATHER, *the* SON *and the* HOLY SPIRIT*"* (Matthew 28:19).

To be a blessing in the life of another is the greatest thing that one can be.

This blessing can begin when you are willingly, voluntarily baptized. Don't put it off! Make your acceptance of HIS gift known, proclaim your faith in JESUS, call on the name of the LORD, and be raised again to a new life in HIS SPIRIT.

My Personal Covenant of Commitment

This day, I wish to establish a personal covenant of commitment with GOD the FATHER, GOD the SON, and GOD the HOLY SPIRIT for the balance of whatever lifetime is granted me by HIS will.

To honor my GOD who frees me, by the atonement of CHRIST, from all my sins—past, present, and future. I ask that it be revealed to my mind, heart, and spirit by HIS HOLY SPIRIT all sins, in thought and deed, that blind and bind me from knowing HIS forgiveness, mercy, and grace.

To engage in a lifestyle pleasing to the LORD and to consciously refrain from any thoughts and actions that may be and are displeasing to HIM.

To always move forward, with time and effort, in a prayer life that is constant and faithful.

To establish a prayer life that focuses upon and touches the lives of those whose life touches mine.

To maintain an intimate personal relationship with the FATHER, SON, and SPIRIT and a GODLY relationship with all others.

To consciously strive to live in the knowledge of HIS presence and to acknowledge HIM daily.

To be obedient to HIS leading through the daily reading of HIS Word.

To being opened to recognize HIS instruction and HIS correction from whatever source HE sees fit in HIS infinite wisdom to place before me.

To be obedient in whatever is laid before me, accepting the goodness and the positive result of HIS will, both for my life and how my life affects the lives of others.

To be able to recognize and repent of all sinful actions.

To daily thank HIM for life and all that HE has provided.

To not ignore nor forsake but to recognize with thanks HIS forgiveness, mercy, grace, and HIS will.

To daily praise HIM with thanksgivings and prayers.

To pray for our nation and revival of GODLY ways, morals, truths, and the knowledge of CHRIST.

To acknowledge HIS supreme sovereignty and righteous judgment, knowing that HE knows and has ordained the beginning and the end of all creation.

This covenant is undertaken with the firm belief that any life without a purpose, a goal, and a faith based on a GODLY foundation is but a house built on sand, destined to collapse. I enter in knowing that this covenant of commitment shall be at times difficult, for faith becomes real and meaningful through constant striving. If faith were easy, it would not be faith.

Therefore, to seek to find GOD and get closer in my understanding of HIM and the reality of my existence, both within the world, HIS creation, and within HIM HIMSELF, is to become a constant act of faith, striving forward and ever upward in my life.

The purpose of life in this world is not comfort nor pleasure or the collection of things but the training, growth, and refinement of my faith to prepare for an eternity with my GOD. This is that which gives life its true meaning and purpose.

I know I shall fail and fail many times, but HE always sees and understands why and comes to pick me up again so that I can continue on with faith growing.

This can and will only be accomplished with a reliance on, by, with, and through GOD in CHRIST and HIS SPIRIT.

_____   _____

(signed)   (date)

To be a blessing in the life of another
is the greatest thing that one can be.
I am present to be a blessing in your life
so that you can be a blessing to someone else.

CPSIA information can be obtained
at www.ICGtesting.com
Printed in the USA
JSHW050736130622
26814JS00012B/62